REWRITING THE NEWSPAPER

REWRITING THE NEWSPAPER

The Storytelling Movement in American Print Journalism

Thomas R. Schmidt

UNIVERSITY OF MISSOURI PRESS
Columbia

The volumes of this series are published through the generous support of
the University of Missouri School of Journalism.

Paperback ISBN: 9780826222244

Library of Congress Cataloging-in-Publication Data

Names: Schmidt, Thomas (Thomas R.), author.
Title: Rewriting the newspaper : the storytelling movement in American print
  journalism / Thomas R. Schmidt.
Other titles: Rediscovering narrative
Description: Columbia : University of Missouri Press, [2019] | Series:
  Journalism in perspective : continuities and disruptions | Revision of
  author's thesis (doctoral)--University of Oregon, 2017, titled
  Rediscovering narrative : a cultural history of journalistic storytelling
  in American newspapers, 1969-2001. | Includes bibliographical references
  and index. |
Identifiers: LCCN 2018059415 (print) | LCCN 2019009460 (ebook) | ISBN
  9780826274311 (e-book) | ISBN 9780826221889 (hardcover : alk. paper)
Subjects: LCSH: Reporters and reporting--United States. |
  Journalism--Authorship. | American newspapers--History--20th century.
Classification: LCC PN4867 (ebook) | LCC PN4867 .S33 2019 (print) | DDC
  071/.3--dc23
LC record available at https://lccn.loc.gov/2018059415

Typefaces: Minion and Trade Gothic

Journalism in Perspective: Continuities and Disruptions

Tim P. Vos, Series Editor

Journalism is a central institution in the social, cultural, and political life of communities, nations, and the world. Citizens and leaders rely on the news, information, and analysis that journalists produce, curate, and distribute each day. Their work must be understood in the context of journalism's institutional features, including its roles, ethics, operations, and boundaries. These features are themselves the product of a history emerging through periods of stability and change. The volumes in this series span the history of journalism, and advance thoughtful and theoretically-driven arguments for how journalism can best negotiate the currents of change.

For Amanda, Teodor, and Maximilian

Contents

Acknowledgments

This book would not have been possible without the support, cooperation, and encouragement of a large and diverse group of people. It evolved from my dissertation at the University of Oregon's School of Journalism and Communication. There, I would like to thank a number of colleagues who believed in the potential of my work when I was only beginning to organize my thoughts: Chris Chavez, Pat Curtin, Gabriela Martinez, John Russial, Kim Sheehan, Carole Stabile, Leslie Steeves, and Janet Wasko. Besides my dissertation work I greatly enjoyed the close collaboration with Andrew DeVigal, Peter Laufer, and Damian Radcliffe. It is customary to thank members of the dissertation committee, but a mere "Thank you" would not do justice to the immense insight, inspiration, and encouragement that I have received from the four scholars on my dissertation team. I want to express my heartfelt gratitude to Lauren Kessler, Gretchen Soderlund, Scott Maier, and Ellen Herman. I admire their scholarship and appreciate their friendship. Lauren supported me all the way since the very beginning of my early graduate studies in literary nonfiction, and the word *advisor* does not even begin to capture her role in how I first practiced and then studied narrative journalism. Seth Lewis and Regina Lawrence joined the University of Oregon when I was halfway through my doctoral program, but they quickly became invaluable mentors who shaped my thinking on this line of research and beyond.

An interdisciplinary study such as this one would not have been possible without the critical input of scholars in a variety of fields. I cannot overstate how much I benefited from branching out to other disciplines and receiving feedback as well as suggestions for further reading. At the University of Oregon, I'm particularly indebted to Alison Gash (political science), Jill

Harrison (sociology), Jeffrey Ostler (history), and Gordon Sayre (English). Encouragement in the early stages of dissertation research is vital for staying motivated and focused. I would like to thank Jack Hart, Mike Fancher, Robert Picard, Victor Pickard, Andie Tucher, Stephan Russ-Mohl, and Rodney Benson, who memorably suggested that I could use him as a foil. I gratefully followed his suggestion. I would also like to thank Vinzenz Wyss for an opportunity early in my research to present my work in Switzerland.

Scholarly associations are indispensable for discussing research and finding an intellectual community. At the International Association for Literary Journalism Studies, I would like to express my gratitude to David Abrahamson, Thomas Connery, Norman Sims, Bill Reynolds, Joshua Roiland, and Tobias Eberwein. I'm particularly indebted to insights and comments from the late John Pauly. The American Journalism Historians Association provided ample opportunities to share my research and receive insightful feedback. And the International Communication Association has become a true intellectual home. There I met Karin Wahl-Jorgensen, whose collaboration to conceptualize journalistic storytelling I greatly enjoyed. Attending conferences of the association also brought me in contact with Thomas Hanitzsch, Folker Hanusch, Jörg Matthes, Patricia Moy, Dhavan Shah, all of whom were supportive of my work. In this context I would also like to thank Nete Nørgaard Kristensen, who invited me to give a talk at the University of Copenhagen and discuss my ideas with faculty and students.

Receiving funding was a crucial part of bringing this book together. I wish to express sincere appreciation for financial support from the Oregon Humanities Center, the Center for the Study of Women in Society at the University of Oregon, the UO Graduate School, the Wayne Morse Center for the Study of Politics, and the Friends of the University of Wisconsin–Madison Libraries. I also benefited from travel grants by the Office of Science and Technology Austria. Funding was most important for being able to do archival research in Washington, DC; Boston; St. Petersburg, Florida; Madison, Wisconsin; and Austin, Texas. In Washington, I am indebted to Evelyn Small. She rescued important *Washington Post* documents from being thrown in the dumpster and shared them with me. My time at the Poynter Institute for Media Studies was especially productive, and this would not have been possible without Roy Peter Clark. He allowed me access to the Eugene C. Patterson papers and other materials at the Poynter Library. He shared personal documents and was generous with his time. Most importantly, he was a very welcoming host.

As much as I enjoyed the archives, I particularly relished talking to some of the people who were instrumental in expanding narrative journalism in American newsrooms. They are too many to list them in this section, but their names are to be found in the references at the beginning of the bibliography. I sincerely thank all of them for their time and patience. I felt honored to hear their stories. And true storytellers they are. I also want to thank some other great storytellers, whose enthusiasm for my project always propelled me forward: my friends Jamie Lay, Lisa Heyamoto, and Todd Milbourn.

It is a rare privilege when scholars whose work is inspiration and motivation for one's own become astute commenters and generous supporters. So I would like to express my sincere gratitude to Chris Wilson and Michael Schudson. Chris was an early champion of my work, read through various drafts, and helped me greatly in turning my thoughts into prose. Michael has also followed my progress from early on and became most influential in nudging me to solve some critical definitional challenges at the very end of the writing process. When I met Tim Vos at the very first academic journalism conference I attended, I enjoyed our conversation but I would have never dared to imagine that he would become so instrumental in getting my work published. I'm very grateful that his confidence in my research led to this publication with the University of Missouri Press, where I've had most pleasant experiences. I would like to thank Gary Kass for his careful reading and smart comments. Dana Henricks did a meticulous job on copyediting the manuscript and offered sharp-eyed suggestions.

My academic career unfolds very far away from my roots in Austria, but my family has shown nothing but love and encouragement for the path I have chosen. My brothers Florian and Sebastian are exemplary in how they pursue their passions in art and athletics, and I have learned so much from them. They have found congenial partners in Hanako and Evelyn. My nephews Fabian and Julian have enriched my life in a way that I did not know was possible. My parents Vroni and Heini have always created a culture of learning and curiosity. They came and visited wherever I studied or lived. They have always encouraged me to follow my curiosity and believe in the value of what I was doing. I hope to pass on a similar philosophy of life to my sons Teodor and Maximilian. Teo entered the world when my dissertation was in the final stages. Maximilian followed when I was finalizing the book manuscript. They always remind me that work is followed by play, adventures, and storytelling. I would also like to acknowledge all the support of my American family, the Peachers. I particularly want to say thank you to

Bonnie, Jim, Heather, Matt, Audrey, and Ethan for all their hours of love and care when looking after our two boys. Finally, my wife, Amanda, is the one person who has seen me work on this book every single step of the way. She cheered me on, lifted me up, and never let me forget that our life is one of wonder and bliss.

Sections of chapter 1 and 5 are revised versions from Thomas R. Schmidt, "Rearticulating Carey: Towards a Cultural History of Journalism," in *Models of Communication: Philosophical and Theoretical Approaches*, ed. Mats Bergman (London: Routledge, forthcoming); and Thomas R. Schmidt, "The Circuit of Culture: A Model for Journalism History," *CM: Communication and Media* 11, no. 36 (2016): 71–88.

Chapter 2 is a revised and expanded version from Thomas R. Schmidt, "Pioneer of Style: How the *Washington Post* Adopted Literary Journalism." *Literary Journalism Studies* 9, no. 1 (2017).

REWRITING THE NEWSPAPER

CHAPTER ONE

Introduction

BETWEEN THE 1970s and the 1990s, American journalists began telling the news by telling stories. They actively reinterpreted, rearticulated, and redefined what journalism in newspapers could look like. They turned away from the "inverted pyramid," a formula that squeezed the most important piece of information into a lead sentence and organized the rest of the material in order of decreasing importance. Instead, reporters borrowed narrative techniques, transforming sources into characters, events into plots, and their own work from stenography to anthropology. This was more than a change in style. It was a change in substance, a paradigmatic shift in terms of what constituted news and how it was being told. It was a turn toward narrative journalism. It was a turn toward a new culture of news. And it was a turn propelled by the storytelling movement.

Narrative journalism emerged from the fringes of newspapers and magazines. It started out as a rebellious act to capture the culture and counterculture of the 1960s. Yet it attracted editors and reporters who wanted to expand the boundaries of newspaper writing, enlarge the appeal for readers, and enhance the mission of the daily press by emphasizing how news affected people. Narrative journalism was built on the belief that journalism had more to offer than detached observation. But it faced formidable obstacles: the professional ideology of U.S. journalism and its "strategic ritual of objectivity."[1] In response, journalists were gradually constructing a set of norms, values, and practices that would challenge ingrained news conventions and gradually establish new ones. Narrative journalism then spread through newsrooms, carried by institutional initiatives and a growing network of practitioners, proponents, and writing coaches who effectively mainstreamed the use of storytelling. Although economic forces exerted competing pressures to sensationalize news content and target an upscale audience, narrative journalists pushed a different agenda. They saw storytelling as a way to revitalize the profession, reconnect with their audiences, and rekindle the artistic appeal of newswriting. This book is about how this story unfolded.

It is a story of institutional change. Storytelling had been popular in the late nineteenth century but fell out of favor until in the 1960s the so-called "New Journalists" (e.g., Tom Wolfe, Gay Talese, Joan Didion, Hunter S. Thompson, Jimmy Breslin) challenged journalistic conventions and reintroduced storytelling to news reporting.[2] When the *Washington Post* launched its Style section in 1969, it deliberately and systematically incorporated narrative techniques into its daily news production. During the 1970s, other newsrooms (e.g., *Los Angeles Times, Philadelphia Inquirer*) were also experimenting with storytelling formats, but it was not until the end of that decade that the newspaper industry as such paid attention. In response to declining circulation numbers, the American Society of Newspaper Editors (ASNE) initiated efforts to improve writing and inaugurated writing awards in 1979. In the same year, feature writing was introduced as a category to the Pulitzer Prizes. By the 1980s, news organizations began pouring resources into the production of narrative news stories. They hired writing coaches, gave reporters more time to work on assignments, and expanded weekend editions by adding narrative stories. Simultaneously, reporters and editors were discursively constructing narrative journalism as a legitimate practice in newspapers. The Poynter Institute, then evolving as the country's leading training center for mid-career journalists, became instrumental in promoting narrative writing at newspapers, and by the 1990s other renowned training institutions, like the American Press Institute and universities (Harvard University, University of Missouri, Boston University), held workshops and conferences about the benefits of storytelling. In the year 2000, a self-declared, yet unofficial "narrative movement"[3] had solidified.

This is also a story about cultural change and journalism's evolving role within U.S. society. Between the 1960s and the 2000s, Americans changed their media diet and amid a growing supply of information options became more discerning about where and how to get the news. Against the backdrop of social and political change, they began questioning institutions and authorities as well as representations of everyday life in the media. In response, the "high modernism of American journalism"[4] started falling apart, leading to confusion about formerly stable genres and changes in the relationship between news consumers and producers. Examining these dimensions is important because it highlights the significance of journalism as a cultural practice. Changes in journalism reflect changes in the way that public debate is shaped. Journalistic norms and values not only structure the work of reporters, editors, and media managers. They also determine what and how readers and viewers learn about the world they live in. The history of narrative journalism, then, provides a distinct perspective to explore how newspapers adapted to the changing lifeworld of Americans in the late twentieth century.

This book supplements prior research about the narrative turn in U.S. journalism and challenges some assumptions about how and why it happened. Some scholars have pegged the emergence of narrative and interpretive forms of journalism to specific events in American postwar history.[5] Others put forward empirical research mixed with philosophical arguments, arguing that news changed from a realist to a modernist paradigm.[6] Still others view narrative journalism as a universal genre that comes and goes in cycles.[7] I subscribe both to the universal importance of storytelling and the validity of general cultural explanations. However, a major objective of this book is to demonstrate the specific impact of journalists and how they mediated and channeled institutional and cultural dynamics. My analysis is based on the view that journalists are, in the words of Christopher Wilson, "cultural mediators" whose "social practice is intimately tied to historical needs, options, and opportunities."[8]

The findings of this book also provide a new interpretation to the emergence of narrative news reporting in relation to the New Journalism. The latter is commonly understood as a body of exceptional works of nonfiction written in the 1960s and 1970s by journalists who became book authors. In this context Michael Schudson argued that "the highly personalistic, openly subjective elements of 'new journalism' had relatively little direct impact on the style of the daily newspapers."[9] My analysis will show that by adopting narrative strategies newspapers created space for personal, subjective, and interpretive writing that incorporated some of the techniques and practices of the New Journalists without giving in to some of their excesses. However, my analysis also challenges the popular belief that it was only a few talented New York reporters (Tom Wolfe, Jimmy Breslin, Gay Talese, Joan Didion, and others) who revolutionized journalism by deciding to employ storytelling techniques in their writing.[10] Ultimately, the findings of this book indicate that the evolution of storytelling in late twentieth-century American journalism was more nuanced, more purposeful, and more institutionally based than the New Journalism myth suggests.

To suggest that narrative journalism expanded between the 1960s and the early 2000s is not to say that it originated then. However, narrative journalism during that time had its own unique characteristics, which this book will parse out. Over the course of a few decades and through the digital transition, narrative techniques and practices have expanded throughout all news sections and all media platforms (print, audio, video). Consequently, narrative techniques have crossed over into the digital realm and, rebranded as storytelling, have come to define many aspects of the media industry.[11] Thus, what started out as a fringe movement has become a mainstream phenomenon.

My analysis does not privilege narrative journalism as the only or the best way to do journalism, but it challenges assumptions of journalism as a uniform and immutable social practice. As Zelizer notes, "[S]cholars have tended to favor uniform, unidimensional and unidirectional notions of how journalism works, which over time have moved further out of touch from the forms that the news has taken on the ground."[12] All too often, the form of news and its inherent properties are assumed in an a priori way. Alternative forms of news that do not align with common notions of a particular and historically contingent form of hard news are sweepingly disqualified as soft news, infotainment, or human interest stories. For example—and it is a symptomatic one—Benson defines his use of narrative journalism thusly: "I aim to call attention to journalistic construction of articles as 'human interest stories' told about nonelite individuals, generally beginning with the lead paragraphs, whose form tends to work against substantial structural analysis or juxtaposition of opposing viewpoints."[13] In Benson's view, these kinds of people-centered stories are inherently incapable of adding social, political, or philosophical analysis to the depictions of personal experiences. It is not my intention to dispute that an abundance of so-called human interest stories lack additional layers of analysis. Yet, an across-the-board assessment like Benson's does not pay enough attention to the nuances in style and form. In this context, my study shows how and to what extent narrative journalism responded to, mediated, and channeled social change. "In the past," wrote Kevin Barnhurst, "each new kind of news may not have made more (or less) sense of the world, but it made *different* sense."[14]

It is not that media scholars have neglected the transformations in the newspaper industry or overlooked the significance of narrative journalism.

My own work builds on extensive scholarship in journalism history, literary journalism studies, and the sociology of news production. To date, however, there is no "institutionally situated history of literary journalism."[15] Moreover, most research on narrative journalism focuses on the magazine and book publishing industry and rarely extends beyond the high time of the New Journalism in the late 1960s and early 1970s.[16] As Forde writes in this context, "[N]o historical study exists from the decline of New Journalism to the present."[17] It is my hope that this book will be a first step to fill some of these research gaps.

Theoretical Approach

As I explore narrative journalism, I think about it in terms of the cultural production of news. By that I mean that journalism encapsulates both aesthetic conventions of representation and social practices of news gathering. My perspective is informed by James Carey, who encouraged journalism historians to examine why, how, and when people accepted the news report as "a desirable form of rendering reality."[18] And he conceptualized the report both as a social form and a social practice, linking aesthetic representation with social interaction. Journalism, in this context, is as "a particular social form, a highly particular type of consciousness, a particular organization of social experience."[19] Too often, these interlinked components of the news production process are treated separately. Therefore, I would like to suggest that the news story is as much an institutionalized expression of journalism as the institutionalized practice of journalism is defined by the constraints of symbolic forms.

Throughout this book I am using the terms "narrative" and "storytelling" interchangeably, but it is worth including a more nuanced definition to delineate what I am talking about and how my perspective differs from other analyses that discuss alternatives to traditional news reporting as "interpretive," "explanatory," or "contextual" journalism. *Narrative*, in its most common sense, is defined as an "account of a series of events, facts, etc., given in order and with the establishing of connections between them; a narration, a story, an account."[20] In the context of journalism, "the term 'narrative news story' refers most broadly to any sort of nonfiction storytelling, but more specifically to a news story that begins with an anecdote rather than a summary lead and then is organized in temporal sequence rather than either by inverted pyramid style or analytically."[21] Depending on how and to what degree news stories employ narrative devices, we can differentiate, as Keren

Tenenboim-Weinblatt suggested, between "different degrees of narrativity" and think about "different journalistic modes—such as soft versus hard news or tabloids versus broadsheets—as different positions on a 'storytelling continuum.'"[22] My particular concern in this book, however, is to avoid applying predetermined definitions of narrative journalism and instead demonstrate how reporters and editors themselves discursively constructed these definitions and made sense of them in their daily work. As a result, my own definition of storytelling has organically evolved from studying the historical emergence of narrative practices and their discursive legitimation. *Storytelling* uses *narrative modes* that can actually appear in different journalistic genres (reportage, report, first-person narrative, etc.) and in different kinds of media (print, audio, video, digital). Nevertheless, the unifying theme is that we can think of any specific form of storytelling as using a specific narrative mode, in other words, "a smaller set of conventions—really a constellation of stylistic effects—that combine together to *elicit* a familiar set of [emotional] responses in readers."[23]

The inclusion of emotion is crucial here. The study of emotional storytelling has been hampered by a false dichotomy between news and human interest stories that permeated some scholarship, reflecting the view that journalism could only do either one or the other. In particular, scholars routinely dismissed the role of emotions as either not relevant or deplorable. As Peters observes, "The concept of 'emotion' is often treated dismissively; a marker of unprincipled and flawed journalism." Yet, this discourse is misguided, he argues. "It rests on an undertheorized conceptualization of emotion that is employed with commonsensical discernment, conflated with tabloid practices, sensationalism, bias, commercialization, and the like."[24] Against this backdrop, it is important to highlight that narrative journalism has added a specific form of emotional appeal, a validation of feelings and how they structure human experiences to American news writing. The narrative approach to news writing affected all aspects of journalists' work: story selection, reporting, interviewing, and writing. As such it constituted a different kind of journalistic epistemology[25] and ultimately led to an emerging framework of norms, values, and beliefs.

In this context it is also important to emphasize that I view the evolution of narrative journalism in newspapers as a process that established new storytelling conventions. By *conventions* I mean a "practice [. . .] commonly adopted in literary works by customary and implicit agreement or precedent rather than by natural necessity."[26] News writing in general is characterized by conventions, and thus the term *news narrative* can also refer to the narrative characteristics of traditional news writing, that is, the constructed character of seemingly natural and transparent news formats such as the inverted pyramid.[27] Narrative devices, as Bird and Dardenne argue, "are used in all news writing, maintaining the illusion that the structural devices used in hard news are merely neutral techniques that act as a conduit for events to become information, rather than ways in which a particular kind of narrative text is created."[28] What the evolution of storytelling and narrative journalism gradually demarcated, however, was the difference between a "news report" and a "news story."[29] The predominant mode of a report is exposition, that is, "[t]he setting forth of a systematic explanation."[30] The predominant mode of a story, on the other hand, is narrative, which is to say, the foregrounding of character, plot, and descriptive detail.

This "customary and implicit agreement" for developing conventions of journalistic storytelling arose from a movement that had originated from diffuse and scattered beginnings but eventually coalesced around common norms, practices, and beliefs. In this study of narrative journalism, I am interested in exploring how a particular group of actors channeled cultural aspects into institutional settings and frameworks. To analyze and explain the evolution of narrative journalism in American newspapers, I am drawing from two theoretical traditions within media studies and journalism research: institutionalism and cultural analysis. In this book I propose a synthesized model that combines elements from both strands of theory.

The two approaches are not necessarily an easy fit. Cultural inquiry seeks to understand the grammar and context of social interactions, while institutionalism is more interested in the manifestation of societal norms, rules, and values in specific entities or interactions. They have different notions of what constitutes continuity, disruption, and change. And their units of analysis do not always belong to the same conceptual level. They are treated as different approaches to studying journalism. Certainly, there are tensions between the two that should not be understated. Schudson cautions that the "cultural" view and the "social-organizational" (i.e., institutional) view are "analytically distinct."[31] He writes, "Where the social-organizational view finds interactional determinants of news in the relations between people, the cultural view finds symbolic determinants of news in relations between 'facts' and symbols."[32] However, even if these views are analytically distinct, it is worthwhile exploring how they intersect and overlap in certain regards.

Specifically, it is worth examining how social interactions are informed by cultural determinants and, conversely and simultaneously, how cultural artifacts and symbols are organized by collective action. Moreover, combining cultural inquiry with institutional analysis is mutually beneficial because this synthesis has the potential to complement the strengths that each of them brings to the table. Institutionalism can offer a toolkit of conceptual mechanisms that explain stability and change across social formations. Cultural analysis provides a sensibility for the "constraining force of broad cultural traditions and symbolic systems."[33] This book will suggest such a synthesis. Blending elements of institutionalism and cultural analysis, I propose to expand the variety of institutionalist models by a synthesized approach called "cultural institutionalism."

The simplistic version of my argument is that institutions and culture work in an intertwined way to structure behavior and attitudes. Moreover, rather than just working from the top down, institutions and culture are shaped by people who enact as well as mediate these higher-order constraints. Like many other scholars, I am thinking about structure and agency as a reflexive process. If I am slightly emphasizing agency more in this book, it is just because I am interested in conceptualizing "institutional emergence,"[34] the process through which social action leads to institutional and cultural change. Put simply, people make organizations, organizations make institutions, and institutions make culture. And again, this process works both ways so that culture affects institutions as they affect organizations and as these structure the lifeworlds of individuals. Cultural institutionalism, then, serves as a theoretically informed strategy to identify the intersection of individual, organizational, and institutional dimensions.

What does a synthesis of institutionalist and cultural analysis look like? How can these related yet distinct approaches blend together? Borrowing a concept from Hanitzsch and Vos, I propose to conceptualize their intersection as a place of "discursive construction," in the sense that journalistic roles are "discursively constituted." As Hanitzsch and Vos put it, "As structures of meaning, [journalistic roles] set the parameters of what is desirable in a given institutional context, and they are subject to discursive (re)creation, (re)interpretation, appropriation, and contestation."[35] It is important, however, that discourse in this context not only refers to a specific rhetoric but to the dialectic relationship between rhetorical and material resources. The mobilization of both kinds of these resources, therefore, demonstrates the efforts of narrative journalists to establish and expand boundaries.[36] Journalism, then, is a process in which journalists discursively construct and mediate institutional *and* cultural norms, values, and routines. News workers actively and subconsciously actualize, enact, and transform practices and formats that are bounded by both institutional and cultural constraints. Yet, they also have the capacity to actively and creatively shape these practices and formats. It is important to note that this process of articulating institutional and cultural elements needs to be understood as a reflexive process. Paraphrasing a famous quote by Immanuel Kant, a cultural focus without institutional elements is empty; an institutional focus without cultural elements is blind.

I understand cultural institutionalism as a model in the sense that it serves as "an intellectual construct which simplifies reality in order to emphasize the recurrent, the general and the typical, which it presents in the form of clusters of traits and attributes."[37] As institutional and cultural dynamics intersect in myriad ways, I would suggest differentiating between three clusters in which news workers articulate and mediate institutional and cultural values. Those clusters reflect different dimensions of what cultural institutionalism in the field of journalism may look like: journalism as cultural institution, journalism as media regime, and journalism as news logic. These clusters will be explored throughout the book, and I will discuss their implications in the final chapter.

* * * * *

In the middle of the twentieth century, newspaper journalism, as Christopher Daly noted, "had a serious problem: most of it was boring."[38] Following the formula of the inverted pyramid, news stories read like telegrams.[39] News reports dutifully chronicled daily events by frontloading the most important information, organizing it as a combination of facts and quotes. Only a few decades later, however, "newspapers have become story papers,"[40] Michele Weldon observed approvingly in 2008. They had rediscovered the power of storytelling and the potential of narrative techniques to make reading the newspaper enjoyable in addition to being informative. From a critical perspective, Rodney Benson asserted that narrative had become "a doxa in American journalism."[41]

How did U.S. newspapers change from gray and boring purveyors of information to lively (and some would argue overzealous) narrators of everyday life? When and why did news stories become less about delivering facts, and more about telling a story? These are the questions I seek to address in this historical study.

Here is the narrative arc of this book: The next chapter examines how the *Washington Post* launched the Style section in 1969 and thus was the first newspaper to deliberately and systematically introduce narrative writing into daily newspaper production. Offering an extensive analysis of internal documents, oral histories, and secondary sources, this chapter presents evidence and makes the argument that the Style section served as a link between New Journalism and a subsequent shift in the newspaper industry toward narrative writing.

The third chapter traces the institutionalization of this narrative journalism in daily newspaper production by analyzing key moments, events, developments, and actors between the late 1970s and 1980s. Examining archival documents and analyzing proceedings as well as publications of the American Society of Newspaper Editors and the Associated Press Managing Editors association, it demonstrates how institutional efforts to elevate the quality of news writing coalesced with individual initiatives in newsrooms across the country to introduce and legitimate narrative writing in daily news production.

The fourth chapter picks up the analysis in the late 1980s. Based on examining archival sources and trade publications, it explores how narrative journalism became a dominating form of news writing in the 1990s. I highlight the role of business pressures but eventually make the point that reporters and editors followed their own, different agenda when they mobilized rhetorical and material resources to define, articulate, and practice narrative journalism in newspapers. Situating the efforts of individuals within an emerging community of practice, this chapter describes how conventions, conferences, and workshops helped construct a common identity, fostered relationships between proponents of the genre, galvanized the imagination of young reporters, canonized theory and practice, and established narrative writing as an institutional fixture in American journalism.

Chapter 5 concludes with a discussion of main ideas and contextualizes them within the three dimensions of cultural institutionalism that I will introduce throughout the book: journalism as a cultural institution, journalism as a regime, journalism as a news logic.

This book tells the story of the storytelling movement in American newspapers—an eclectic group of artists in reporters' clothing, anthropologists of the changing cultural landscape, analysts of American minds and mores at a critical moment in time. It was a movement with no single path, but many directions. I am calling it a movement because in all their diversity, reporters and editors put forward a reform agenda for journalism around the unifying idea that storytelling had something to contribute to reporting reality, that it would have something to say about the human condition that was lacking in traditional newspaper writing. Over time, practitioners and proponents of narrative journalism formed a professional community, benefited from a changing institutional infrastructure, and established novel ways of knowing and writing. Eventually, they fundamentally changed how Americans read the news and learn about the world they live in.

CHAPTER TWO

A Rough Draft of Culture

The *Washington Post* and the Invention of the Style Section

BEFORE THE *WASHINGTON Post* "Style" section became a success story, it was a messy affair. And before it became a prototype for narrative journalism in U.S. newspapers, it was a bold experiment in storytelling that initially chased as many readers away as it attracted. Some would complain that the new form of narrative storytelling was "in poor taste."[1] Some advertisers would find the stories too long, too tedious, and too little focused on local events and fundraisers. Within the newsroom, the section would sometimes be perceived as "a haven for amateurs, freaks and advocates."[2] There was editorial infighting and tensions between female editors from the former women's pages and the staff who were brought in to design a modern, audacious form of storytelling and criticism. There was sexism. Most importantly, *Post* publisher Katharine Graham would be sporadically impatient with the product and deplore both its form and its content. Disagreements over the direction of the Style section would lead to the only heated fight she ever had in her special professional relationship with executive editor Ben Bradlee, who had conceived the section. Graham would badger Bradlee to the point that he famously told her, "Take your finger out of my eye."[3]

And yet, seven years after its launch, the Style section would be called Bradlee's "clearest personal monument."[4]

Before turning to the *Washington Post*, however, it is necessary to briefly recall what the landscape of newspaper journalism looked like in the postwar years. The eventual success of the Style section was all the more notable because most U.S. newspapers during the 1960s were not known for their creativity. In the two decades after World War II, content innovations were not high on the agenda of editors and publishers. By and large, they focused on economic growth and business as usual. The newspaper industry benefited from the overall expansion of the U.S. economy and reaped the benefits of the boom years. In 1945, the average metropolitan daily published twenty-two pages. By 1965, the average number of pages had increased to fifty. Advertising content grew faster than editorial content, but the latter grew to almost twenty pages, up from about twelve two decades earlier, an increase of 60 percent.[5] In 1965, an editorial in *Editor and Publisher* declared, "The newspaper industry business in these United States today is growing, healthy and prosperous."[6]

Yet, underneath this optimistic outlook, a number of trends were developing that would challenge the newspaper's hegemonic role and eventually force the industry to fundamentally modernize the ways in which it was presenting the news. As more and more Americans moved to the suburbs, the metropolitan dailies were confronted with changing needs of their readers and their advertisers. The baby boom generation was coming of age in the 1960s and proved to be a challenging audience to attract. The growth of circulation was barely keeping up with the overall growth in population. Television made a big leap in the 1960s, demonstrating that it was not only distracting the masses but also informing instantaneously when national events (e.g., the assassination of President Kennedy) and international crises (e.g., the war in Vietnam) unfolded. Moreover, American society as such was undergoing fundamental social, cultural, economic, and political changes: the civil rights movement, youth and counterculture, the women's movement, the rise and fall of New Deal progressivism, and the beginning of a conservative revolution.

In some ways, the *Washington Post* in the mid-1960s was like other metropolitan newspapers. It was focused on breaking news, daily events, and the proceedings of government and politics. "The Washington *Post* that Ben Bradlee took over in 1965 was a good and genteel liberal newspaper," wrote David Halberstam. "It was not as good as its reputation. It always seemed on the verge of becoming a great newspaper but it was not yet a great paper."[7] Bradlee wanted to stir things up and found favorable conditions that set the *Post* apart from most newspapers. The *Post* had become a market leader after World War II after a time of initially competing with three and then two local newspapers (*Washington Star, Washington Daily*). As the number one newspaper in town, the *Post* benefited from the postwar trend of advertisers and local businesses funneling their advertising dollars toward the leading paper at the expense of the competitors. This was a result of television becoming a more popular advertising venue, which generally diminished the share of newspapers in total advertising. As newspapers across the country gained a monopolistic position in their markets, they often gave in to complacency, inertia, and resistance toward innovation. Not so the *Post*. In Washington, DC, the *Daily News* did not fold until 1972 and the *Star* existed until 1982. As a result, the *Post* had incentives to offer interesting editorial content and increase circulation with marketing and sales.

In addition, the *Post* was not only competing on the local level. Bradlee wanted to take on the *New York Times* on the national level. In the late 1960s, this competition was uneven. The *Times* had more reporters, more correspondents, and an established position as the paper of record. It was an editor's paper, meticulously crafted to cover "all the news that's fit to print." In a mix of admiration and envy, people at the *Post* called this "cruising speed." In contrast, the *Post* "did its best work in spurts, then often seemed to fall back in exhaustion and torpor."[8] Nevertheless, the underdog status spurred the *Post* to think about innovation, and its looser organization allowed for more experimentation. It was considered a writers' paper, meaning that reporters had more leeway and were less constrained by organizational routines, all of which attracted talent, especially when it meant working in the capital, a city that was changing fast.

Washington, DC, grew significantly in the 1960s. As the federal government expanded, more people moved to the metro area, filling jobs in the city and putting down roots in the suburbs. The business side of the *Post* boasted that the paper was serving an area that was "the fastest growing (first in the top ten U.S. markets)," "the most affluent (highest per household income)," and "the best educated (highest percentage of high school and college graduates)."[9] In addition, the cultural scene was exploding. Museums and galleries sprung up, the Kennedy Center opened, and pockets of a bohemian artistic scene developed. Washington was highly segregated but offered more opportunities for a black middle class than most other cities.

The growing metropolitan population also reflected larger trends of social and cultural changes throughout the country. The 1960s brought social unrest, the civil rights revolution, and a growing sensibility for inequalities in U.S. society. They also brought backlash, political violence, and the rise of a conservative movement eager to roll back progressive reforms. And the decade brought an unprecedented increase in affluence, education, and leisure time. While keeping loyal readers was one concern, winning new ones was another. And the new and growing target audience had a name—the baby boomers. James Baughman noted that "[a]s the cohort born between 1945 and 1960 entered adulthood, newspaper circulations, contrary to industry expectations, began to drop. Between 1974 and 1977 circulations fell from

63.1 million to 60.7 million. Studies suggested that adults under thirty were the least likely to read a newspaper."[10] Bradlee understood that the *Post*, in order to reach this new generation growing up in the tumultuous 1960s, had to offer a "more irreverent, spicier" form of journalism.[11] Born after World War II, the baby boomers now were the fastest-growing segment of the population in the nation. In the Washington, DC, area alone they amounted to almost eight hundred thousand.[12] They were well educated and not all that interested in the traditional lifestyle of their parents. As their interests revolved around clothes, records, books, and leisure, media outlets were scrambling to meet their needs. They were coming of age reading edgy magazines like *Esquire*, *New York*, *Rolling Stone*, or the alternative (and dissident) press.[13] Also, from an advertising standpoint, they were a highly desirable audience.[14]

Meanwhile, one of the most consequential of these postwar demographic trends was the increase in women working for pay. After a dip following the end of World War II, when many women had to yield their jobs to returning veterans, female employment rose constantly. In addition, more and more women working outside the home were married. Their numbers rose from 36 percent in 1940 to 52 percent in 1950 to 60 percent in 1960—and to 63 percent in 1970. The "most important cause of the trend was the desire of married women to enter the market," noted James Patterson. "These were not women starting careers when they were young; they were housewives belatedly finding work, much of it low-paid, in order to help ends meet in their homes."[15] This changing role of women started to become an issue in newspapers, not just in terms of content but also in how the papers conceptualized their female readership. As a result, any effort by newspapers to adjust to these complex dynamics of changing audiences and their needs would require a delicate balance between attracting new readers while not alienating loyal ones. The Style section did not find that balance right away. In fact, far from being a fully developed model at its inception, the Style section came together in a process of trial and error, reflecting contested notions of journalistic values, professional practices, and readership expectations. It is easy to overlook how groundbreaking and revolutionary the Style section was when it began.

"For and About Women"

Traditionally, newspapers had a peculiar way of reporting about women and addressing their female readers: they had distinct women's sections. At the *Washington Post*, the section was called "For and About Women." Under the leadership of Marie Sauer, the women's pages of the *Post* had made tentative steps toward reaching a more diverse female audience (instead of solely focusing on the wife/homemaker role). Although women's sections typically had to fight for attention in the newsroom environment, "For and About Women" was well established and supported, not least because publisher Katharine Graham was a careful reader.[16] Sauer, a demanding boss deeply respected by the women reporters working for her, ran the women's pages "almost like a separate newspaper."[17] She was driven by feminist beliefs, yet reluctant to align herself fully with the emerging women's movement.

> I always thought women could do anything they wanted to do—from running a home to running a city or a nation. I was always for the [Equal Rights Amendment], equal pay, child care, etc. . . . I thought women should have any jobs they wanted. I thought many more women should run for the Presidency, Congress, local offices. But I believed that any woman, if she wanted to, had the right to concentrate on child rearing and community and cultural activities.[18]

While one of the main tasks for reporters in the women's section was covering society events in Washington, Sauer required her staff to think about their reporting from various news angles. As Judith Martin recalls, "Miss Sauer—we never called her anything else—would bark that the society beat was no different from the police beat and send us to White House, State Department and embassy parties to quiz the newsmaker of the day."[19] With this strategy, Sauer validated the women's reporting as serious journalism, undermined the stigma of soft news, and created opportunities for women reporters to feel empowered. Despite the progress under Sauer, however, her approach to providing news for women seemed to be out of touch with the social and political environment during the late 1960s. Bradlee was not a feminist, yet he was attuned to the changing gender roles. In retrospect, he acknowledged that he was "sexist" and credited his first wife, Tony Bradlee, for influencing his change of mind. He described her as "an early, sort of a modest bra-burner, and [. . .] on the streets all time [*sic*], protesting the war."[20] Changing the women's section was not one of the first projects that Bradlee took on after becoming executive editor in 1965. But three years later and after expanding the newsroom staff, Bradlee wanted the women's pages to disappear. In a memo he wrote to Graham and his top editors, he suggested that the "[w]omen's section as it is now constituted be abolished."[21]

The representation of women and their interests was a major concern, but there was also the big issue of improving the "readability"[22] of the paper.

Prior to Style, items like reviews (art, movie, theater), television listings, news stories about the cultural scene, and features were scattered throughout the paper. Thus, there were also pragmatic reasons for combining the women's pages with the arts section while seizing the opportunity to reconceptualize the coverage of stories that did not fit into the national or metro sections. Essentially, Bradlee wanted a back-of-the-book section as was customary in magazines such as *Time* and *Newsweek*, where he had been bureau chief in Paris and Washington, DC, before coming to the *Post*.

If Bradlee was the visionary of the Style section, David Laventhol was its mastermind. He was one of Bradlee's favorite assistant managing editors and had experience in designing newspapers as daily magazines, first at the *St. Petersburg Times*, later at the *New York Herald Tribune*. In the fall of 1968, he visited the *Los Angeles Times* and the *Detroit Free Press* to gain insights about new lifestyle and women's sections. Comparing the *Post*'s content to the other papers, he noticed that the society coverage in the women's section held up well, while coverage of newly developing areas like fashion, consumer issues, entertainment, and especially pop culture needed improvement. The biggest takeaway from this reconnaissance trip was that Laventhol saw great potential for a section that was tentatively called Life Styles. "What surprised me," he wrote to Bradlee, "was the limited thinking that is going on in this area." He reported that the *Los Angeles Times* was thinking about innovation, too, but did not develop a concept beyond combining the entertainment coverage with the women's section. Later he recalled, "[A]s part of my development effort, I read the *Times*, visited the Times Mirror Square, spent considerable time with [editor] Nick Williams and others, and stole a lot of ideas."[23] Not mentioned in his report but widely known during that time was the fact that the *LA Times* had begun experimenting with the idea of making a newspaper more like a daily newsmagazine.[24] Supported by publisher Otis Chandler, who had taken over the family business in 1960, and conceptualized by editor Nick Williams, the *Times* promoted interpretation and analysis.

Laventhol praised Dorothy Jurney of the *Detroit Free Press* as "probably the brightest person in the U.S. about conventional womans [sic] editing," but added, "that ends it."[25] The only real innovative new section in American newspapers, in Laventhol's estimate, was a Monday supplement by the *Chicago Tribune* called "Feminique." Conspicuously absent from Laventhol's review of women's sections was Charlotte Curtis, the women's page editor of the *New York Times* who emphasized issue-oriented coverage but also had made a name for herself as an acerbic commentator on the rich and famous.[26] Laventhol concluded his original report to Bradlee by saying, "I'm still trying to bring thoughts together, but I think that Fashion [a preliminary title for the section] in its original sense—the current styles of life—is what is the key to the whole thing."[27]

Breaking up the women's pages and conceptualizing a new section allowed the *Washington Post* editors to do something that was rarely done in newspapers during that time: redefine the purpose, the audience, and the format of daily print journalism. Laventhol laid out the concept in the fall of 1968. The new section, he wrote, "would be oriented to the Washingtonian—male and female, white and black, suburbanite and citydweller [*sic*], decision-maker and home-maker. Reports and evaluations would probe the quality of this life—and the kind of things happening elsewhere that affect it." It would introduce a revolutionary format, innovative layouts emphasizing pictures, drawings, and color. The section would have its own front page and throughout, "[s]tory, picture and headline would be unified to stress thematic goals." As for the focus of the section, "[p]eople would be stressed rather than events, private lives rather than public affairs." Laventhol further explained that the section would expand traditional notions of arts and entertainment coverage to include "styles of life," covering a wide spectrum from fashion to popular culture. "Reportage of what's happening . . . the scene . . . in clothes, and also tastes, language, manners and mores, life furnishings, parties, entertainment, books, records, etc." Of particular concern would be how readers spend their time when they were not working. "The leisure revolution is transforming America, but it is virtually undeveloped by newspapers."[28]

This conceptual framework constitutes more than an isolated example of editorial innovation. It illustrates how journalists were actively channeling, mediating, and interpreting cultural transformations to find a place in the newspaper for them. Their efforts illustrate how journalism, at its most general level, is a cultural institution in that it provides rules and practices for exchanging, conveying, and receiving information, analysis, and other cultural formats (entertainment, service, etc.) in a structured way. Although journalism comes in variations—both over time and across different cultures—it speaks to a universal desire for hearing from and connecting with other people by telling stories.[29] Humans are storytelling animals, and as storytellers journalists fill an important role in complex societies. Journalists are cultural agents, tapping into a cultural repository of artifacts and practices to shape and sustain public debates in a variety of contexts. They define their self-understanding by relying on a professional ethos that assigns journalists a particular function in society—the fourth estate, the watchdog, and so on. They find legitimation and take pride in emphasizing that their work makes public debates more informed, transparent, and accountable. Journalists also play an active role in offering reassurance and familiarity, credible answers and explanations for complex issues.[30] News production is more than the basic process of bringing a particular journalistic artifact into being. Rather, it is a cultural process that is informed by the interaction between intra-organizational practices and larger cultural forces—distinct ways of life within which journalistic forms need to resonate.[31] In sum, journalists take part in constructing, upholding, and sometimes subverting the normative and cultural contours of the communities they serve (or claim to serve).

In this journalistic effort of collective meaning making during the late 1960s, the term *life style* played a particularly important role. As Leo Bogart noted, the term emerged in the advertising business in the 1950s and then gained currency in the sales departments of magazines. "In its original usage 'life style' describes a subtle complex of designations (including social class, ethnic origins, area of residence, position in life cycle, and so on) that corresponds to a distinctive set of tastes and patterns of consuming goods, services, and leisure time."[32] In fact, when the *Post* reconceptualized the Style section, it followed a path that special-interest magazines had charted throughout the 1960s. These new magazines focused on topics from fashion to food and from sailing to sewing, encompassing a wide range of leisure activities. They were springing up in the 1960s and contributed to the precipitous decline of general-interest mass-market publications.[33] Ultimately, this was a first step into segmenting the general audience into subgroups for targeted marketing and advertising, a development that would now spread to the newspaper world. Yet in contrast to magazines, the *Post* had to be careful not to lose its appeal to a mass audience. Its target audience, as identified by Laventhol in the quote above, was Washingtonians. What the paper could do, however, was to offer segmented content within its pages, geared toward the diverse interests and backgrounds of its readers.

In fact, with their women's sections, newspapers had been segmenting their audience already, if only in a crude way. "Women were treated exclusively as shoppers, partygoers, cooks, hostesses, and mothers, and men were ignored," Bradlee wrote in his autobiography. "We wanted to look at the culture of America as it was changing in front of our eyes. The sexual revolution, the drug culture, the women's movement. And we wanted to be interesting, exciting, different."[34] Despite this emancipatory rhetoric, however, it was no accident that change started with dismantling the women's section. It was the place of least resistance. However much Marie Sauer tried to empower the women on her staff, it was part of a gendered newsroom, with more stereotypes and less value attributed to "women's issues." And as much as Sauer emphasized hard-news reporting, the section still reflected a general stereotype of women's news, namely that it was soft "human interest" journalism, a form of newswriting fundamentally cast in gendered terms and viewed as inferior and negligible.[35] On the other hand, that inferior status also provided opportunities to break with some of the routines of news writing. "The point is that what we call the women's pages aren't so heavily weighed down with unchangeable definitions of what they must contain and how they must present it," Nicholas von Hoffman, an early star of the Style section, told a room full of women's page editors in the early 1970s. "They are in the best position to show the rest of the paper what you do when most people get their first news, and the news they believe most, from radio or TV." Yet, von Hoffman argued, it was not only the content that distinguished women's sections from the rest of the paper. Also the form of writing set them apart because they were "freed from the conventional forms of presentation, the three or four W's, pyramid construction, all the things that allow us to kid ourselves into thinking formula writing is good writing, or even good journalism."[36] It was this relative lack of conventional news writing that created an opening for the new section to become more daring, more experimental, and ultimately more narrative than the rest of the newspaper.

The Comeback of Storytelling

The first Style section appeared on January 6, 1969, and led to a general reorganization of the *Post*'s daily presentation.[37] Both in terms of graphic layout and editorial content, the section was a significant departure from the past. The first edition of the Style section featured the first woman to be listed on the FBI's "Ten Most Wanted" list. Two days later, on January 8, the front page of Style led with a story titled "Life Styles: The Mandels of Maryland," a profile of Marvin Mandel, Maryland's then newly chosen governor, and his family.

> About 6:30 in the morning, Marvin Mandel, who was chosen Governor of Maryland yesterday, rolls out of the double bed and heads for the bathroom

at the head of the stairs (a small bathroom, in light blue tile, with three tooth-
brushes hung from little holes around the edge of a cup sconce, a plastic curtain
concealing and also indicating the bath-shower, and a neat medicine cabinet
containing a tube of Prell, a can of shaving foam, a slot for used razor blades,
and three or four jars and boxes but no medicines, not so much as an aspirin)
and shakes off the five hours of sleep which is all he usually gets or needs.[38]

The story goes on to describe a day in the life of Governor Mandel: when
he leaves (at eight in the morning); when he returns home (at seven or eight
in the evening); what he watches on TV ("any damn thing that's on"); what
he reads (everything from *Time* magazine to the Book-of-the-Month selection); what he drinks ("Bourbon is Mandel's drink, but he rarely takes more
than two, even during the conviviality of a legislative session"). As a family
portrait, the story also quotes the governor's wife ("He couldn't find a thing
in the kitchen") and his daughter ("They are very understanding parents.
[. . .] For instance, they have never set up a curfew").

The story was novel both in terms of news content and with regard to
the story form.[39] In contrast to previous profiles in the women's pages, this
article was a family portrait, describing not just the first lady (as would have
been the customary approach in the women's pages) but the whole family
dynamics, including the grown-up children. Thus, the content was a novelty. However, this story also offers interesting evidence that illuminates how
the Style section incorporated narrative, documentary techniques in daily
newspaper reporting. Thus, the form was a novelty, too. With regard to the
story form, the profile employs an ironic tone, suggesting to the reader that
the depictions of this picture-perfect family should be taken with a grain of
salt. Signposts of irony are strewn throughout the text,[40] but the writer's tone
of bemusement reaches a climax at the very end:

> Assembling in the living room, the Mandel family posed for a portrait, smiling
> gently and flashing unanimous gray-green eyes. Behind them stood a pair of
> marble stands topped with ivy bowls, a glass dish of wrapped hard candy by
> the sofa and, next to the fireplace, a small table bearing a vase of plastic yellow
> roses.

This article is an excellent example of how the narrative frame affects
the representation and interpretation of the subjects. To understand how
radically this approach departs from previous conventions in the women's

pages, one can look at a story that ran just a few days before the Style section was launched. Under the headline "Mrs. Onassis Explores Scenic Charms of Greece," the article began: "Mrs. Aristotle Onassis and her children sightsaw the Greek isle of Lefkas on New Year's Day, clambering up steep hills and riding donkeys to view the beautiful scenery."[41] Instead of a deferential treatment, the Mandel story portrayed the mundane details of the governor's life and did not hold back on irony (some readers took it as cynicism). In contrast to depicting the bucolic life of the rich and the famous, this story was rich (almost to a fault) in what Tom Wolfe called "status details,"[42] specific observations or descriptions that provide clues to a person's socioeconomic status and personality. The story shows the private side of a public figure, but by using a narrative frame of irony, the author also cautions the readers not to trust everything in this staged setting and encourages them to look behind the façade of the polished politician. A few years later, the Mandels would again take up quite some space in the Style section, and by then, the image of the wholesome family had fallen apart. The governor left his wife for another woman and she had refused to leave the governor's mansion for five months.[43]

Emphasizing the function of the narrative frame is important in this context because this story form breaks away from a traditional news form that adheres to presenting the news in a supposedly neutral way.[44] The two frames differ in what they focus on. The narrative news frame responds to the question "How do we live?" The straight news frame, in contrast, answers the question "What happened?" While the straight news frame prioritizes a particular event, the narrative news frame zeroes in on the context.[45] The personal point of view (as told through a third-person narrator) of the narrative news frame reveals a private life not so different from that of ordinary citizens. In the case of the Mandels, this rhetorical move decreases distance and difference, humanizes the subjects, but also mildly ridicules their personal tastes. This difference in style also reflects an evolution of different news values. The private becomes political and is subsequently scrutinized for consistency with or deviation to the public image. Even though the profile is more descriptive than narrative, it employs typical traits of narrative storytelling, especially the use of status details to craft a character.[46] Seeing and describing the world through the lens of narrative technique is very different from applying the "5 W's" approach of traditional news reporting.[47] Of course the Style section did not invent the narrative form of news reporting, but it systematically incorporated it into daily newspaper production.

As such, it expanded the space in which the newspaper offered stories about people and how they lived.

Some aspects of this focus on people and how they lived were already an essential component of the women's pages, and it is also important to acknowledge this continuity. In fact, Style and its narrative approach validated and elevated earlier forms of "soft journalism." Capturing motivations and moods of people in the news was a crucial element of the women's pages. Style reporter Judith Martin wrote, "As we used to say, 'We don't just cover a story; we surround it.' Our assignment was to produce sidebars that supplied the details and the participants' motivations and moods—the color—that gave meaning to the dry news accounts that were then standard in the A section."[48]

The Style section continued with this approach but expanded its reach from covering "women's issues" to general news, with a particular emphasis on trends and profiles. Focusing on popular culture and capturing the zeitgeist of the 1960s was a relatively new concept for most newspapers of this era, but also indicative of their changing role as cultural institution. Newspapers were reluctant in adapting to the changing cultural climate and the growing competition of television. Nevertheless, innovations in newspaper content and design had been going on for years and in a variety of places. Of particular importance was the *New York Herald Tribune*. Before it ceased publication in 1966, it was a laboratory for new approaches to daily journalism. Part of its innovative spirit was to bring techniques from magazine journalism to the newspaper, a strategy that was personified by John Denson. He had improved the standing of *Newsweek* and closed the gap to its dominating competitor *Time* before taking over as editor of the *Herald Tribune*. (Bradlee was bureau chief at *Newsweek* under Denson, about whom he said, "He taught me the sizzle is important, not just the steak.")[49] Denson made the paper more accessible and readable by emphasizing that the format ought to accommodate the news, not the other way around. He introduced catchy headlines, typographical innovations, horizontal instead of vertical design, and allowed for plenty of white space to focus the reader's attention. The content got more sparkle and the writing became more interpretive. James Bellows, his successor, toned down the sensationalism but followed Denson's approach to make the paper more modern, more sophisticated, and more fun than any other American newspaper of that era. Ben Bradlee wrote in his memoir, "Every newspaperman worth his pad and pencil had mourned the passing of the *New York Herald Tribune* in 1966. Wherever they worked, journalists envied the *Trib*'s style, its flair, its design, its fine writing, its esprit de corps."[50]

Bellows created an atmosphere that gave young, untested reporters like Tom Wolfe and Jimmy Breslin free rein to experiment with storytelling formats. Under Bellows's reign, the *Herald Tribune* emphasized elements of news reporting that indicated the shift toward a more narrative style of journalistic storytelling: describing people like characters, not sources; using sensory detail for descriptions; telling stories instead of writing news reports.[51] In an internal memo, national news editor Dick Wald spelled out some of the characteristics. To tell the truth was the reporter's chief obligation, he wrote. Yet, he emphasized that "the truth often lies in the way a man said something, the pitch of his voice, the hidden meaning in his words, the speed of the circumstances." Wald advocated for writing with "a strong mixture of the human element" and articles that were "readable stories, not news reports written to embellish a page of record."[52] Despite all this innovation, however, the *Herald Tribune* folded in 1966 and thus called into question the very possibility whether such a different style of writing could be sustained in daily newspapers.

One of the young staffers in Bellows's newsroom was David Laventhol. "I don't think they ever said, 'Hey, we're in the television age; we've got to put out a different kind of newspaper,'" Laventhol later told a historian. "But they had things like a news summary on page one. They had a tremendous amount of rewriting—a lot more like a magazine in many ways than a newspaper."[53] After the *Herald Tribune* ceased publication, Laventhol carried over some of its philosophy to the *Washington Post*.[54] In the aforementioned concept for the Style section, he laid out how the purpose of the new section—focusing on people and private lives—also required a new style. "Direct reports, with lots of quotes and hard, specific detail, would be emphasized," he wrote. "The tone would be realistic, not polyannish [*sic*]. Clarity would be the guiding principle of the writing style; it would be bright without being flip; sophisticated without being snobbish; informed without being 'in.'"[55] This description is noticeable because it indicates elements of the New Journalism—the combination of "hard, specific detail" with a "realistic" tone, yet also defines the particular approach of the *Post* and accentuates the contrast to some of its potential competitors and the freewheeling experimentation of some New Journalists like, for instance, Hunter S. Thompson. When Laventhol rejected a Pollyannaish tone, he seemed to push back against other approaches to lifestyle sections with lighter fare and fluffier prose. The other juxtapositions are instructive as well. Even if Laventhol does not mention any specific media from which he wants to set the *Post*'s new section apart, his characterizations can be understood in light of the media ecosystem of the late 1960s. It appears that Laventhol wanted to position the new section as different from other models of that era like *Esquire* (flip), the *New York Times* (snobbish), and *New York* magazine ("in"). Thus, Laventhol provided a blueprint for a journalistic style that used some of the elements and approaches that would later be defined as New Journalism.

Despite literary precursors in the late nineteenth century, the so-called New Journalism of the 1960s had marked the beginning of a new era of narrative journalism in the United States. By adapting the style and technique of fiction writing to journalistic work in newspapers, magazines, and books, the New Journalists expanded the range of journalistic writing that resonated with mainstream audiences and triggered interest from commentators and critics. Writers like Gay Talese, Tom Wolfe, and Joan Didion built their literary reputation in magazines and then received lucrative book deals. Novelists like Truman Capote and Norman Mailer ventured into nonfiction and gave the emerging genre cultural cachet. Ultimately, Wolfe would coin the term *New Journalism* as an idea "to give the full objective description, plus something that readers had always had to go to novels and short stories for: namely, the subjective or emotional life of the characters."[56] The writers of this informal collective accentuated journalism as storytelling, simultaneously embracing their role as cultural interpreters. As such, their activities were "a response to a broader interpretive crisis in the journalism profession that was decades in the making."[57]

At the same time, however, the inside perspective of the *Washington Post* illustrates how, despite similarities to the magazine world, the environment at daily newspapers was much more restrictive and structured than at monthly publications. As much as Wolfe and others identified characteristics of the New Journalism, these descriptions pertain to the writing in magazines and books. The specific context of newspapers—including their norms, values, and culture—stood in contrast and presented different challenges. When Robert Darnton reflected on his time as a newspaper reporter, he wrote, "Copyeditors seem to view stories as segments in an unremitting flow of 'copy,' which cries out for standardization, while reporters regard each piece as their own."[58] These entrenched practices, then, inhibited innovation at newspapers in the 1960s. The *Post*'s example shows us how they were gradually overcome.

The Style section, as envisioned by Bradlee and designed by Laventhol, transposed and adapted the idea of journalists as interpreters of cultural trends from magazines to the newspaper. In doing so, it carved out a space for narrative writing to appear in a daily newspaper, de facto (re)introducing a then-forgotten form for telling the news. The narrative form broke with conventions and established a novel, if not unprecedented, cultural form of news. As such, the Style section actively shifted culturally determined genre conventions, allowing reporters to experiment with literary forms that challenged traditional forms of news writing. What this means is that journalists took on the role of, in Christopher Wilson's words, "cultural mediators" whose "social practice is intimately tied to historical needs, options, and opportunities."[59] "Mediators" in this context refers to a dialectical process: reporters were borrowing ideas and techniques from other authors, thus reflecting stylistic conventions that were circulating in neighboring fields. At the same time, they were also makers of culture, adopting and reinterpreting those conventions to transform the practice of news writing.

The storytelling itself was not new, of course. But the context in which it appeared was. A brief example illustrates what institutional resistance against narrative form in the news sections looked like. Prior to Style, the *Post* had some writers that were experimenting with narrative style in the news section. Nicholas von Hoffman had made a name for himself as voice of the youth and counterculture within the *Post*.[60] He had also pioneered the use of narrative techniques in daily newswriting at the paper.[61] One episode from 1968 illustrates how controversial this kind of approach was. Covering the funeral of Martin Luther King Jr. in Atlanta, von Hoffman opened his story by writing, "The Rev. Dr. Martin Luther King Jr. led his last march here today. He was in a cherrywood coffin, carried in an old farm wagon to which were hitched two downhome mules."[62] The story was published on the front page, against the express wishes of deputy managing editor Ben Gilbert, who said, "It was not a lead-the-paper story. It was a feature."[63] This was the kind of dichotomous logic that Style challenged and eventually overcame. It demonstrated that news and features were not opposites. Rather, it showed that features carried news and that news could be featurized and thus narrativized.

Nevertheless, daily production of news differed from the magazine world from which the narrative writing was imported. Magazines had to plan months ahead to meet their particular production needs. Journalist and scholar Garry Wills described this process as "lead time."[64] He wrote, "The best editors made a virtue of necessity—they learned to stand off from the flow of discrete items filling daily newspapers, to look for longer trends, subtler evidence. They developed an instinct for the things a daily reporter runs too fast to notice." The *Washington Post*, however, had to figure out a way to do both: fill the daily news hole and look for "longer trends, subtler evidence." In practice, this meant that the new section needed organizational routines capable of reconciling those competing demands. As it turned out, those routines would take years to take shape and they would only solidify after a period of tumultuous leadership struggles, internal strife, and external criticism. As Laventhol summarized the state of Style after three months, "STYLE is. But what it will be continues to be a necessary debate."[65]

The Impact of the *Post*'s Organizational Culture

Conceptualizing the Style section was one thing, putting it into action yet another. As editors and reporters were experimenting with story formats and content, the evolution of the new section was followed with great interest by publisher Katharine Graham. Despite a certain involvement in the development of the new section (Graham sat in on brainstorming sessions), she was not all too pleased once it had rolled out. Some of the stories she found "tasteless," "snide," or "grisly."[66] Then the pendulum would swing in the other direction. "Clothes, fashion, interior and the frothy side of the paper are all taking a hosing," she wrote in a memo to Bradlee. "In view of the fact that a good hunk of our income comes from retail stores and the broad base we are always bragging about, I am really getting quite fed up with the really heedless egg headedness [*sic*] of STYLE."[67] Graham was actively lobbying for a female editor of the entire section (not just the women's news) "because as long as you have culture-happy editors who dislike and don't want women's news in, you are going to have this situation continue." And she added, "I can't see why we have to build ourselves a structure in which we have to fight and plead and beg to get into the paper (and I have never said this before in 5½ years) what I quite frankly want to have there."[68] Looking back, she wrote in her autobiography, "I became more and more distressed over the direction the new section was taking, but I was unsure how to criticize constructively something I wanted to improve."[69] Graham complained to Bradlee so persistently that one time, as previously noted, he yelled at her: "Get your finger out of my eye!" As they both recounted later, this was the only heated fight they ever had.[70] Graham backed off, but her concern for advertisers—who worried about losing the women's section, an important

opportunity to connect with female customers—and the traditional readership base raised the stakes for the section to succeed.

The Style section was embedded in a particular newsroom culture that
Bradlee created. He governed the newsroom with charisma, magnetism, and
a visceral presence that would instill awe and send chills down the spines
of his reporters.[71] With an "absolute sense of stage presence" he would walk
the newsroom, prowling for the newest gossip, as his reporters and editors
remember.[72] The biggest validation was a slap on the back, a quick comment
like "a helluva story," the undivided attention of the boss who was said to
have the attention span of a gnat.[73] Bradlee was equally powerful when communicating his disapproval. "What the fuck are you doing?" he would berate
reporters with characteristic vulgarity.[74] The biggest punishment, however,
was when reporters realized that Bradlee was ignoring them. Fully aware
that they were craving his attention, Bradlee would turn his back or avoid
eye contact. "He could be really cruel and obtuse," remembers Henry Allen.
"He was like a cat playing with a mouse sometimes."[75] Bradlee ran the newsroom on a star system[76] and pushed his staff to compete with each other,
pitting editors against editors and reporters against reporters.[77] He called
it "creative tension."[78] It was a "piranha atmosphere," the longtime editorial
writer John Anderson said in an interview with David Halberstam. "It can be
uncomfortable as hell, but it may also be very good for people. And Bradlee
is very good at making them feel that they're right on the edge."[79]

The guiding principle for Bradlee was impact. As he described his vision in the late 1970s to Chalmers Roberts, a *Post* reporter and designat-
ed historian of the paper: "I want to have some impact in this town and
this country. [. . .] I want to know they are reading us. Impact."[80] The most
prominent examples of creating impact were publishing the Pentagon Papers in 1971 and then, of course, Watergate and the reporting that led to the
resignation of President Richard Nixon. But Bradlee's craving for impact
was not just motivated by a particular political stance or an overarching
moral vision.[81] He just immensely enjoyed good stories about power, people, and gossip.[82] Typically, the stories that he appreciated the most were
tales about winners and losers, one person's rise and another one's fall, human drama expressed in terms of individual bravery or tragedy.[83] In other
words, Bradlee appreciated the power of storytelling. With this affection
Bradlee set the tone for the Style section (as with the rest of the paper), even
if he did not get involved that much in the day-by-day operations. As Larry
Stern, one of Bradlee's best friends, noted in the late 1970s, Bradlee "is a

good newspaperman but not a sustained one. He doesn't follow through."[84] Bradlee had a vision for Style but it was intuitive and not informed by a conceptual framework or specific guidelines. He encouraged and advocated a sensibility for more personal, magazine-like stories and enjoyed good writing. What that looked like in a particular context was for the editors to decide and achieve. A story succeeded when Bradlee felt that it reached a wider audience and got people talking.

Attracting talent was costly, but Bradlee had the full support of Katharine Graham and became a tough negotiator in dealing with the business side of the paper. As a result, the news budget more than tripled between 1966 and 1969, rising from $2.25 million to $7,295,087.[85] "It was a wonderful, expansive time," wrote Halberstam, "when everything was possible, when everyone was a star, when, if *The New York Times* was larger and bulkier and more respectable, there was a belief that the *Post* was better, livelier, more exciting. It was the successor to the *Herald Tribune*, a writer's paper."[86]

One of the first reporters specifically hired for the section was Myra MacPherson. Her professional biography reflected the constraints that women reporters were faced with during the postwar years. After having worked on the student newspaper at Michigan State University, she went looking for a reporting job on the city desk of various newspapers but only got offers for writing for the women's pages. At the *Detroit Times*, she covered a wide range of topics, including sports. Reporting on the Indy 500 in 1960, she was neither allowed in the press box nor Gasoline Alley. Bradlee offered her a position in the women's section, assuring her that after three months the section would change into the Style section. When MacPherson said that she could not work full-time because of her two young children, Bradlee responded, "For Christ's sake, the last things those kids need is you around the house full-time."[87]

Michael Kernan was an example of Bradlee's strategy to put some of the *Post*'s best writers into the Style section. Bradlee described him as a "poet in newspaperman's clothing."[88] After thirteen years of being editor of the *Redwood City Tribune* in California and a year in London, Kernan had landed at the *Washington Post* in 1967. He started out as a city editor, but because of his elegant writing he was assigned to the Style section.[89] The Style section also offered opportunities for young women reporters, among them B. J. Phillips, Judy Bachrach, Lynn Darling, and Megan Rosenfeld. The most prominent one in the early years was Sally Quinn, also one of the first hires for the new section. She was hired without previous journalistic experience but quickly rose from a neophyte party reporter to a star writer specializing in chatty, yet illuminating personality profiles.[90] Later she would become Ben Bradlee's wife and a fixture in society news.

The Style section's diverse composition caused a variety of complications, some of which had to do with the former staff from the women's section. Most of the assignment editors were from the women's section, while the reporters were not. Moreover, the section was understaffed but overstretched for daily events. This created friction in all areas of the daily production, from the selection of topics to the planning and writing of stories. These problems deepened after Laventhol left to become editor of *Newsday*, especially during the time when the leadership was divided between Elsie Carper and Thomas Kendrick. Carper was a veteran reporter from the women's section, Kendrick an aspiring editor from the metro section. Carper had the ear of Katharine Graham, Kendrick the support of most reporters. Tensions between the two escalated.

These conflicts reflected the intertwined dynamics of office rivalries, gender issues, and generational tensions. An instructive document capturing these dynamics comes from a young reporter who summed up her impressions as she was leaving the paper. Comparing Kendrick and Carper, she wrote, "I think the section needs a man with children and a well-adjusted family life instead of . . . women." About Kendrick she added,

> I am particularly heartened by his sensitivity to the women's lib thing. He is the only really major editor in this place not to scoff and make jokes about it. And he is quite serious in listening and trying to learn what we're talking about when we say no more pseudo-achiever stories, etc. [. . .] and demeaning adjectives, etc. More than any man at the Post, I think he is capable of handling women as people—which is what the whole idea of Style was supposed to be about, stopping the old way of reporting nonofficial, often distaff Washington. (n.d., anon.)

Evidently, these impressions only reflect the point of view of one reporter. Nevertheless, they illustrate how the Style section was a place that simultaneously encouraged women reporters to speak out while also creating an environment that pitted veteran women editors against young women reporters. These internal conflicts were embedded in a newsroom environment of considerable sexism. "There [at the *Post*] were no women assistant managing editors, news desk editors, editors in financial, sports, or the TV magazine, or in the Sunday 'Outlook' section, no women in foreign bureaus, and no women sports reporters."[91] Women at the *Post* were arguing that this lack of opportunity for women in the newsroom also affected the coverage in the paper.[92] In a memo to the *Post*'s management, the women at the newspaper expressed their discontent:

> Many stories considered expendable deal with social issues of interest to the general reader but are given short-shrift in this male-oriented, politically attuned newspaper. The issues of women's rights, health, consumer news, day-care, abortion, and welfare are examples of stories not being adequately covered and displayed. The *Washington Post* would be a better newspaper if it used the talents and perspective of more women in assigning and evaluating stories on such issues.[93]

Words were followed by actions when women at the *Post* filed a complaint with the Equal Employment Opportunity Commission. In 1974, it concluded that the *Post* concentrated women reporters in certain sections (Style, Metro), had no women editors or assistant editors, and paid men more than women doing comparable work.[94]

In contrast to gender, race was a less obvious issue, but it was all the more striking because the section was designed to explore black culture and lifestyles. Hollie West was the first black reporter in the Style section, transferred from the city desk to become the jazz critic. "I didn't feel isolated or alone," he recalled later. "Not in any sense." There were other black reporters on the paper that he bonded with. In the Style section, West was eventually tasked with writing about African American lifestyles. "Yes, being black was fashionable at the time. They wanted pieces about the black culture."[95] In 1970, Kendrick suggested and succeeded to make West a general assignment reporter. "We must plug into the black community," Kendrick wrote, "and cannot afford having our only black reporter so restricted." He also conceded that "coverage of black stories other than those involving entertainers" had become "[b]etter, though not adequate."[96] Nevertheless, even two years later Bradlee stated that there was "no reporter in Style specifically assigned to cover black lifestyles," and that he would also be opposed to such an assignment. "We are trying in Style, as elsewhere to avoid black-on-blacks reporting."[97] Then, after mounting complaints about the lack of black and female staffers, the *Post* hired Dorothy Gilliam to become the first African American and the first black woman as editor at the Style section. In an oral history interview, she recalled: "I sort of saw what I wanted [as] my goal, to bring some coherence to black culture, so I was able to make a number of hires and get a lot of, I thought, quite interesting things into the newspaper."[98] Style was more diverse in terms of race and gender than any other desk at the *Post*. Nevertheless, the struggle for adequate representation and involvement would not be resolved until later in the 1970s.

Within the organizational culture of the newsroom, the quality of writing was of special concern to Bradlee and his top editors and vividly debated in internal communications. One particularly illuminating document is a memo that Eugene Patterson, then managing editor, sent to Bradlee in June of 1971. Not only does it highlight the significance of writing at the *Post*, it also demonstrates how debates about the New Journalism found their way into the newsroom. Patterson was responding to an internal discussion about creating a statement of principles or set of standards for reporting and writing. Citing a piece from Tom Wicker in the *Columbia Journalism Review*, he argued against a singular institutional or professional formula. Instead he emphasized the importance of creating and nurturing an environment for reporters as artists.[99] Then Patterson discussed a piece by Tom Wolfe about the New Journalism in the *ASNE Bulletin*, an excerpt of Wolfe's eponymous book which was published later, saying, "[I]t lays out exactly what constitutes the New Journalism, in which I happen to believe." He embraced Wolfe's view that new nonfiction was as much about substantial and insightful reporting as it was about skillful writing. Patterson concluded his memo by making a case for incorporating some of the New Journalism techniques into the daily newspaper production.

> We need fewer exhibitions of moralistic, committed, romantic thoroughly conventional essay and more courage to do an *artist's reporting of universal reality*, not personal commitment, and the skill to put it together. We are talking about artists, which is what The Washington Post ought to be about, and not about tin ears who try to write rules.[100]

Patterson's view was just one piece in a larger context of internal debates, many of which are not documented in a paper trail, but it encapsulated and promoted particular elements of the *Post*'s culture that were constitutive for establishing the Style section. It was also consistent with key elements of Bradlee's newsroom culture: good writing and substantial reporting, a star system based on skillful writers, and a desire to stay ahead of current trends in journalism. Eventually, the Style section would come together along the lines that Patterson had envisioned: without a dogmatic formula but based on a shared understanding to do "an artist's reporting of universal reality." Moreover, Patterson's intervention was also one of the earliest signs pointing at the larger significance of organizational practices that were consonant with Style's subculture. Far from being relegated to the margins of the newsroom, the style that Style cultivated was embraced and ultimately expanded into other sections of the paper. "One of the things I would most like to see us undertake is an effort to make the news more meaningful and understandable in human terms," wrote Richard Harwood, then head of the national desk, in 1974. "We need more of that in the national report. We need more profiles and character essays of the men and women who people our pages; Style has no monopoly on that."[101]

Most of the writers were very much aware that they were part of an endeavor meant to shake up traditional journalistic patterns of reporting and writing. What they were doing, as Sally Quinn said looking back, "threw a grenade into old-school reporting."[102] Many of them considered themselves to be reporters *and* writers. Often their inspiration came from the emerging New Journalism. Judy Bachrach recalled, "I wanted to make everything I wrote a short story. Like in fiction. Like Tom Wolfe when he first started out, or Gay Talese. Those were the people we not only studied at the Columbia School of Journalism, but they came to us and talked to us. That was really cool. They really influenced us tremendously."[103] Henry Allen admired Tom Wolfe's "in-the-know wise guy treatment combined with brilliant prose," his "esoteric words," and how he was able to "play it high and low."[104] As he remembered it, when he arrived at the *Post* he realized that "the Style section is full of people who had been reading the same stuff."[105] Leonard Downie Jr., who was never part of the Style section but had been at the *Post* since 1964 and would succeed Ben Bradlee as executive editor in 1991, said, "We were all aware in the newsroom of the New Journalism. I remember looking for Tom Wolfe's pieces in *New York* magazine. I remember looking for those things and I remember people talking about it. So there was a kind of awareness of what was going on."[106]

Over time, Style became notorious for its tone, which would run the gamut from snarky to satirical, from ironic to judgmental. At the same time, especially women reporters developed a reputation as insightful and incisive profile writers. The combination of Sally Quinn, Judy Bachrach, Myra MacPherson, and Nancy Collins was called, both reverently and disparagingly, "Murderer's Row."[107] Katharine Graham recounted a conversation with Henry Kissinger when he said: "Maxine Cheshire [the *Post*'s gossip columnist] makes you want to commit murder. Sally Quinn, on the other hand, makes you want to commit suicide."[108] This kind of reporting was not only revolutionary for a "family newspaper" but also for a city that had been known as the "graveyard of journalism."[109] And it proved to be challenging for some parts of the audience.

A Shifting Audience

In the first days of the Style section, the *Post* was inundated with negative phone calls from readers. The new section "lacks feminine touch" and is "too sterile and too masculine," complained one reader. Another caller demanded "more 'women as women' stuff." And then there was a number of readers that were mainly one thing: confused.[110] Particularly strong reactions came after the profile of Governor Mandel of Maryland. The detailed description of the governor's bathroom was so shocking to a wider audience that the story was soon referred to as "the medicine cabinet profile."[111] Letters to the editor show that some readers were unsettled by the story's descriptive details and its narrative lens. "Really now," Cheryl A. Skuhr of Arlington wrote. "Surely there must be more interesting things to write about the Mandels other than their type of bathroom!" For Catherine Kaufman, the article was "cheap and vicious." She called it "a hatchet job 'exposure through intimacy' [. . .] that should be done on someone who deserves it, not on a man just starting out as a very public figure." And Dorothea Beall of Stevenson, Maryland, added, "Of all the things that I am interested in knowing about the new Governor of our State of Maryland, what is kept on his bathroom shelves is really at the bottom of the list."[112]

These early reactions certainly resulted from a variety of motivations, but they also indicate that the narrative style was irritating to a significant group of readers. Arguably, these readers were not so much puzzled about detailed descriptions as such. What they were really upset about was finding these stylistic elements in the *newspaper*. They would probably not have been so surprised had this been a magazine story or a fictional narrative. Apparently, their expectations of *what* a newspaper should report, and *how* it should report, were upset.

"[J]ournalism history," Andie Tucher writes, "requires the historian to address not just how the journalism worked but also how its audiences judged acceptability and what they understood their journalism to say about their relationship with the world."[113] Against this backdrop audience research has amply demonstrated that consumers are more than passive recipients of journalistic formats. They actively interact with the news they receive and shape it according to their own needs. Journalism is not only a reflexive process between symbolic forms and social practices; these social practices themselves are a reflexive interaction between the producers and the consumers of news. Consumption encompasses a wider area of practices than merely focusing on actions such as buying a product or receiving a message. The news consumer is not a passive victim of propaganda but an active agent of appropriating and constructing meaning in the practice of his or her everyday life. "[M]eanings are not simply sent by producers and received by consumers but are always *made in usage*."[114]

In this context, readers' responses to the Style section point to a shifting social landscape and also a moment in time when some audience members expressed evolving attitudes and expectations toward newspaper content, while traditional readers actively resisted. Loyal female readers of the women's pages were appalled by the new direction. Younger readers (especially but not exclusively women) enthusiastically embraced the new format. Initially, advertisers sided with the traditional audience and rejected the new section. Eventually, however, they realized the potential of catering to a younger, more consumerist clientele, advancing the segmentation of audiences by focusing on a narrow, yet desirable segment of the population. So how did readers make sense of the new format and what does that tell us about the shifting cultural ground of the 1970s?

The women's pages might have appeared anachronistic to Bradlee and his leadership team, but the section had its loyal readership. Moreover, these female readers had specific expectations about content and form as well as the way in which the women's pages fit into their daily lives and political beliefs. Edith Fierst of Chevy Chase, for example, was not happy with the Style section. "For many years," she wrote, "it has been my ungrudging custom to surrender the first section of *The Washington Post* to my husband when he arrives for breakfast about 5 minutes after I do, and to read the Women's section instead. Now this tranquil arrangement is threatened, as morning after morning I find nothing to read in the Women's section."[115] She went on to complain that many articles embraced viewpoints of the New Left, noting that "most Americans do not subscribe to it." In her view, the "steady diet of articles blaming the 'establishment' for everything, often in a smart-alecky way, [is] neither enlightening nor interesting."

For some traditional readers, the new direction of the Style section betrayed a tried-and-true template for combining entertainment with what they perceived as a female perspective. "Your now-retired editor knew her women," wrote Mary L. Anderson in a personal letter to the *Post*. "She knew that even some of her highly educated women subscribers who read the editorial pages and columnists first, would then turn to her pages and be purely female." Anderson added that women readers enjoyed the lighter fare of parties, gossip, and home stories. And she was unapologetic. "Why? Because most of us are leading fairly hum-drum lives, and it was fun to leave our own tedium for a few minutes each day and read about people who could go places and do the things we can't." For readers like Mary Anderson, one task of the newspaper was to provide escape, and that escape was defined in gendered terms. Her comments also point to a quasi-aristocratic critique of the *Post's* turn toward documentary realism. "[W]ith a steady diet of coal miners' widows and mothers of deserters and Von Hoffman's snide comments, we go back to our own labors more depressed than before we stopped to read the paper. The news columns tear us apart enough. Is it a sin to look for whatever frivolity is still around?"[116]

It was not just the content that elicited criticism. The form of Style, particularly the narrative reporting of news stories, caused consternation as well. In a personal letter to the *Post*, reader Martha Grosse argued that covering society events was like covering sports and that many readers were particularly interested in the play-by-play descriptions. She deplored the fact that Style was abandoning this approach and instead focused on "feature" stories. "What you have done is cut out the *news*—and these parties and Embassy affairs *are news*—in favor of a magazine type approach [in] articles on everything and everybody," she wrote. "If I want to read this type of stuff I buy a magazine, what I look for in the daily paper is reporting of *daily news*, and in this case news of women type social affairs in Washington."[117]

Over time, however, the complaints decreased and readers began to embrace the content and form of the Style section. Reader Margaret E. Borgers responded to critics of the new direction and praised the new section as a "daily treasure," adding, "I, for one, am greatly flattered by *The Post's* innovation, with its implicit statement that women might be interested in something besides debuts, weddings and diplomatic receptions."[118] The self-image of this new demographic and its expectations for coverage in the *Washington Post* can be gleaned from an early letter to the editor from one such female reader, praising Nicholas von Hoffman—the first star writer of the Style section:

We are not young radicals. We are the forgotten middle class lot C. Wright Mills has dubbed the voiceless and unrepresented. We are not snobs, nor are

we the Silent Majority. We try to keep informed. We write our Congress-
men. [. . .] We read the editorial page first. We have participated in demon-
strations and worked for our candidates. We are for the equality of women
and minorities, against the war, support liberalized abortion, lowering the
voting age, equality for all in basic human needs such as medical devices,
food, jobs and a breatheable [sic] environment. The list is endless, as are the
problems we face and attempt to solve. At last we have a voice through Mr.
von Hoffman.[119]

But while some of the baby boomers—male and female, as this letter
suggests—were highly invested in the political debates of the day (Vietnam
war, student protests), others shifted their attention to an increasing industry of leisure activities, supplementing the larger trend toward consumerism. David Abrahamson has shown how cultural changes like consumerism
and leisure propelled the growth of special-interest magazines in the 1960s.
"Empowered with affluence and education, happy to be enlisted in an as-
cending social class, free of the conformist strictures of the 1950s, but cut off
from traditional communal sources of identity and social class, many turned
to active leisure pursuits to add coherence and meaning to their lives."[120]
What this meant for a daily newspaper like the *Post* were opportunities to
explore these changes, blending narrative descriptions with social commentary. Michael Kernan, especially, became an expert in chronicling trends of
the 1970s such as consumerism and self-improvement.[121]
    In contrast to magazines, with their increasing specialization on niche
audiences, the *Post* was a general-interest newspaper. So the focus on particular groups of readers raised practical and conceptual issues. In its effort
to keep traditional women readers, yet also win young and African American readers, the *Post* was dealing with competing goals. Katharine Graham
remarked in a memorandum, "If we want young black readers, do we want
them on the same page as women and at the expense of our *base* readers?"[122]
As already mentioned, the columns of Nicholas von Hoffman became a
cause célèbre. The *Post* leadership was grappling with the polarizing nature
of his writing. Von Hoffman "is writing in a field where nobody else has
really ventured for the purpose of trying to give their readers some grasp of
the youth phenomenon which very few of us have fully understood," wrote
Patterson in a memo. "We print him in the belief that it is better to know
what is in the minds of people who we may not agree with rather than not
to know."[123] Another dilemma was that as much as the *Post* wanted the Style

section to appeal to both men and women, it originally kept "Woman" in the masthead, which further supported the notion that Style was just another women's section. Only after persistent lobbying from Elsie Carper, Bradlee and Patterson agreed to change the masthead from "Woman" to "People."[124]

Conceptions of the audience also changed because newspapers were no longer just competing with each other for readers. They also needed to come to terms with the fact that a growing number of people turned to television for their news. The transformation was gradual, yet fundamental. After television's growth in the 1950s and its coming of age in the 1960s, it played a major role in people's news diet. The year 1964 was the first in which more respondents named television as their major source of news than named newspapers (55 percent versus 53 percent).[125]

Of course the makeup of the audience was of particular interest to advertisers. Initially, they were anxious about losing a clearly defined target audience (women) without gaining access to the desirable, yet elusive, baby boomers. Advertisers also complained that advertising in the Style section was not as effective as in the women's pages. In response, the business side of the *Post* demanded that Bradlee and Patterson create enough space for "women's news" so that advertisers would have an environment for specific women's ads.[126] Ultimately, however, advertisers embraced the new concept and the *Post* continued to profit from increasing ad buys. Its advertising lineage in the DC metro area increased from 60 percent in 1971 to 72.1 percent in 1978.[127]

Writing in Style

After about five years, the basic elements of the Style section were in place: a consistent philosophy, a reliable workflow, and productive collaborations between reporters and editors. Thomas Kendrick, who had been instrumental in shaping Style into a cohesive unit as section head, summarized the state of Style in a memorandum in late 1973. It is worth quoting the conclusion of this memo in its entirety as it identifies key ingredients of a new narrative news logic that had taken hold at this point. News logic can be defined as "a form of communication and as a process" through which news outlets "transmit and communicate information."[128] However, instead of accepting that there is a unitary news logic in journalism, we can distinguish various configurations of formats and practices that constitute news logics—"the rules or 'codes' for defining, selecting, organizing, presenting, and recognizing information as one thing rather than another."[129]

Kendrick emphasized the importance of keeping the section experimental; he advocated the serious, hard-news relevance of its content; and he made a case for embracing the narrative news logic as a promising way to capture the human side of the news. He wrote:

> Style's original concept holds. A number of subsidiary definitions of Style's role have been forged since its inception and this is as it should be. For many, these definitions seem hazy and that too, perhaps, is as it should be. It may well be a fatal error to define Style's role too strictly. The freedom to experiment, to gamble, to make mistakes (but not to repeat them) is basic to Style's charter. Such freedom is necessary to avoid the cardinal sin of dullness.
>
> Finally, *there should be an end to the attitude that Style is a soft, feature section* that can be ignored or curtailed in the crunch. *It feeds information that directly affects how people spend the leisure time that now occupies one-third of their lives.* Style's quick success and broad readership are evidence that its focus on people tapped an unfilled need. People are going to have more leisure time in the years ahead and their cultural interest will continue to expand. The political-governmental tunnel vision that this paper sometimes exhibits should not blind us to the possibility that our readers may be telling us that "people" are as important as "facts," that Style's fare is much more than luxury.[130]

When the *Washington Post* published an anthology of the best stories from the Style Section in 1975, it was a testament to the evolution of the section into a cohesive entity that was actively promoted as innovative news content.[131] When Kendrick moved on to become the director of operations for the Kennedy Center for the Performing Arts in 1976 and Shelby Coffey took over the leadership of the Style section, Style was established. In addition, the *Post* had reached the peak of reputation and cultural cachet. When stars and high society flocked to the Kennedy Center for the premiere of *All the President's Men*, the movie that lionized the *Post* and its reporters Bob Woodward and Carl Bernstein for their Watergate coverage, it was obvious that the *Post* had made the step from reporting the news to being in the news. Within ten years, Bradlee had elevated the *Post* from a "swamp town gazette"[132] to the most talked about paper in the country. Moreover, Bradlee became a person of interest himself and his relationship with Style star writer Sally Quinn only added to the mystique. David Remnick put it this way:

> To understand the scale of Bradlee's achievement, it is important to know something about the mediocrity with which he began. The Washington *Post*

in 1965 not only had no claim to rivalry with the New York *Times* but could not even claim to be the best paper in its city. Ever since the *Post* bought out the *Times-Herald*, in 1954, it had been profitable, but as an editorial enterprise it still was simply not competitive. It was, like most newspapers everywhere, pretty awful.[133]

Writing for *Esquire* in early 1976, James Fallows portrayed Bradlee and the *Post* in all their glory. "In the past ten years," Fallows wrote, "Bradlee has remade *The Post* in his own image, making it, at different times, the most exciting paper to work on, the most interesting one to read, and the one from which wrongdoers had most to fear."[134] As mentioned previously, Fallows called the Style section Bradlee's "clearest personal monument"[135] at the paper. He praised Style's approach for going beyond mundane gossip. "It carried symbolic gossip," he wrote, "the novelistic details, the significant anecdotes that tell everything about the way the world works. So much of life within the government, so much of Washington society, could be explained as a game of manners—and Style did try to explain it.[136] By describing and "explaining these games of manners," the *Washington Post* went beyond the traditional role of the press and its task to provide, in the words of the *Post's* early publisher Phil Graham, a "first rough draft of history." When the Style section highlighted the lifeworld of politicians and people alike, attuned to changing attitudes, values, and practices, it provided a first rough draft of culture.

Despite Style's influence, however, some of its writers were dissatisfied with the lack of professional recognition, specifically that there was no Pulitzer award for feature writing. "The age of the mere color stories and human-interest sidebars ended when Style was born," wrote Style writer Henry Allen in a memo to Bradlee. "Feature writers get read, get famous, get people buying newspapers, and should get their own Pulitzer."[137] Bradlee agreed with Allen's analysis, pledged a new effort to change the situation and then had an opportunity to do so as a member of the advisory board of the Pulitzer Prizes.[138] Records indicate that there was significant resistance toward elevating feature writing into its own category. Some board members feared that this "would touch off an avalanche of entries, many of them of dubious quality. Every feature about a fireman rescuing the neighbor's cat would come in. Also the usual features about babies, bright children, rural teachers, reformed alcoholics and fallen stars."[139] This characterization reflects the widespread skepticism toward stories that did not fit the mold of hard news, but also more specifically how feature journalism was deemed as something of lighter quality and less public importance. That kind of resistance was also palpable within the *Post*. Some editors criticized that too many stories deal with fads and "lack a sophisticated and critical tone," missing "the larger element around us."[140]

When the advisory board assigned Bradlee and Patterson (who had moved on to become the editor of the *St. Petersburg Times*) to describe if and how feature writing could be included in the Prizes, it was Bradlee who pushed for a separate category. Rejecting other suggestions that wanted to fold feature into an existing category, Bradlee lobbied for a Pulitzer Prize in Feature Writing. In a letter to the board, he wrote that "some of the best writing in the press today is being done in this category. Not a paper worth its salt has not started a feature section during the last two decades. Profiles, life-styles, features . . . these are the lifeblood of a newspaper. These are the categories where the fine writers are found. And no Pulitzer to urge them on to greater heights."[141] On January 25, 1977, the advisory board voted to establish a new Pulitzer Prize category of Feature Writing and a few weeks later adopted a definition and description that was worded by Patterson: "For a distinguished example of feature writing giving prime consideration to high literary quality and originality."[142] The first Pulitzer Prize in Feature Writing was awarded in 1979 to Jon Franklin of the Baltimore *Evening Sun* for "Mrs. Kelly's Monster," a narrative account of brain surgery.

Conclusion

The Style section continued to be the "prototype for daring, literary-minded newspaper feature sections throughout the country,"[143] but in the early 1980s the *Washington Post* also suffered the biggest embarrassment of the Bradlee era—the Janet Cooke scandal.[144] The fabricated piece about an eight-year-old heroin addict did not appear in the Style section, but it had larger implications for the practice of narrative journalism. The scandal pointed to some potential pitfalls of narrative journalism (i.e., ethics of reporting, sensationalism, melodrama), which would become topics of heated debates throughout the 1980s and 1990s.

Nonetheless, by introducing and supporting narrative techniques, the *Washington Post* played a significant role in changing both the form and the practices of daily journalism in newspapers. Practices changed because the routines of reporting and interviewing for narrative had to be accommodated by the infrastructure of daily newspaper production. At the same time, the form of narrative journalism also evolved since it anchored narrative innovations in a journalistic mindset and journalistic ethics that differed from the magazine or book industries. "[Style stories] should be evaluated not as literature but as journalism with all its inherent strengths and faults," Kendrick wrote in the aforementioned introduction to the anthology of Style stories. "They carry both the bite of immediacy and deadline warts, the punch of individual perception and flaws exposed by time's perspective."[145]

Eventually, the *Post*'s innovation had significant effects on American newspaper journalism in the 1970s. Style provided a template for documentary writing and role models for narrative journalism, and laid the groundwork for a broader effort to incorporate magazine-like storytelling in daily newspaper production. As other major American newspapers began developing their own "style" sections throughout the 1970s (*Los Angeles Times*, *Miami Herald*, *New York Times*), their indebtedness to the *Post*'s trailblazing became obvious.[146] This transformation created occupational structures and literary incentives (such as that Pulitzer Prize in Feature Writing) so that young, talented writers would seek out careers in journalism. It also led to the formation of a readership that would embrace narrative storytelling as an integral part of their daily newspaper diet.

The next decade would bring an expansion of narrative journalism, but also charges by some that narrative writing signified a triumph of style over substance.

CHAPTER THREE

Storytelling Goes Mainstream

Narrative News and the Newspaper Establishment

ONE MIGHT THINK that newspapers have always taken great care of the writing on their pages. One might think that words have always been carefully crafted in a medium whose editors aspired to be the keepers of the public record. One might think that there has always been high esteem for turning rich facts into vivid prose so that newspapers would sometimes become a training ground for authors who would leave a lasting imprint on the literary world. But despite this lore, the reality in the late 1970s was a different one. "God knows most papers," wrote Stuart Dim of the *Charlotte Observer* to fellow editors in 1977, "are too frequently dull, dull, dull, and on most days aren't worth the money they charge. We sometimes ought to pay readers to read us."[1] In addition, most newspapers did not pay much attention to training reporters or offering resources for improving their writing skills. When Ron Goble, managing editor of the *Times-Delta* of Visalia, California, was asked to study training programs in newsrooms, he concluded, "Training. That's something too many newspapers lack today and something ALL newspapers could improve upon. It would solve a lot of our writing and editing woes."[2] But not only that. As some leading editors were realizing in the late 1970s, it could also help solve the industry's readership woes.

These woes originated from a structural problem: While the population was growing, circulation was stagnating. Throughout the 1970s the adult population in the United States grew by 19 percent and the number of households increased by 25 percent. Newspaper sales, however, did not keep up. In fact, throughout the decade the readership gap only widened.[3] So when the leaders of the American Society of Newspaper Editors (ASNE) met for their board meeting in Honolulu in 1976—debating issues of circulation, advertising, and budget departments—Tim Hays, the editor of the *Riverside (CA)*

Press-Enterprise, spoke up. "We are neglecting a job we supposedly are best equipped to handle," he said. "That is, improving writing in our papers. If we can't do that, we might as well quit."[4] What followed was an unprecedented effort to leverage the institutional power of ASNE and its sister organization APME (Associated Press Managing Editors association) to provide resources, infrastructure, and professional recognition for enhancing the craft of writing in U.S. newspapers. In 1977 ASNE officially launched a writing improvement program "in the belief that if we can improve our writing, theoretically that would help improve readership."[5] It inaugurated writing awards for newspaper journalists, furthered research and training, and created platforms such as reports and newsletters for promoting writing skills and best practices.

Initially, these efforts were simply focused on improving the clarity and correct use of the English language. Over time, however, and in combination with individual writing initiatives that were springing up across the country, this industry-wide initiative fostered the conditions for the story-form and narrative journalism to take hold and grow in daily newspapers. What started out as a plan merely to improve clarity in writing resulted in a fundamental rethinking of storytelling in newspapers, ultimately involving not only new narrative techniques but also reporting and writing approaches that would engage readers emotionally. Eventually, as this chapter will explain in more detail, a distinctive focus on the practices, ethics, and implications of narrative writing emerged along the following lines. At the most basic level, writing programs challenged the traditional article *form* based on the inverted pyramid, and instead promoted classical storytelling techniques as alternative ways of presenting the news. Thus, improving writing led to a diversification of story forms and formats. At the same time, challenging the traditional article form also meant questioning the traditional *content* of news and what constituted news in the first place. As more and more journalists became engaged with narrative storytelling, they actively promoted story forms that prioritized the human angle, the "soft" side of hard facts. What they wanted was to imagine a different kind of news that was more attuned to readers, to the human condition in general, but without resorting to yellow journalism, sensationalism, or tabloidism. In order to find that balance, journalists and editors had to reconcile the "demands of narrativity" with the "demands of reality"[6] as they were constructing and legitimating storytelling in the production of news. What they eventually did was to collectively construct a distinct organizational logic for writing news, an interlinked set of journalistic forms and practices combined with a different professional epistemology. As a result, a new, narrative news logic took shape, changing the very culture of news writing.

This news logic, the institutional evolution of which the chapter will parse out, is characterized by combining interpretive and explanatory elements with literary techniques and emotional engagement, establishing a news culture that challenged traditional concepts of objectivity and detachment.[7] As such, the narrative news logic was more than an interpretive turn, connected to but different from contemporaneous shifts toward analytical and explanatory journalism.[8] Moreover, narrative journalism encouraged reporters to expand their range of reporting skills by engaging with their sources more emotionally than journalistic routines would allow. As reporters were turning their reporting into prose, matters of narrative form—the narrativizing of events and experiences—brought to the foreground what had been eclipsed from journalism as the occupational norm of objectivity had expanded earlier in the twentieth century, namely, it brought back notions of interpretation, subjectivity, and empathy.

Since this narrative news logic was being collectively constructed and since it was developing across organizations, yet another transformation began to unfold. As more and more newspapers were adopting the *practice* of narrative journalism, as they were mainstreaming the narrative techniques, storytelling gradually affected the very *purpose* of journalism. Narrative journalism as a way of emotional storytelling advanced the idea of humanizing the news, centering reporting and writing around how individuals were affected by events, social forces, and government actions. In doing so, narrative journalism expanded the notion of information delivery to include what Hanitzsch and Vos have called "the domain of everyday life," the area in which "all persons must manage their emotional state and negotiate their identity. These everyday activities are not without implications for politics and public life, but also not reducible to the political."[9] This change, therefore, was an institutional change toward a news regime that challenged dominant assumptions of objectivity and established a new form of news, new journalistic roles, and a new epistemology that linked the private sphere with public life.[10]

Before examining this institutional change, however, it is important to briefly sketch my understanding of news regimes as historical formations for journalism. Institutions constrain actors by rules, practices, and narratives.[11] A particular formation of journalism can be described as a regime. In Williams and Delli Carpini's definition, a media regime is "a historically specific, relatively stable set of institutions, norms, processes, and actors that shape the expectations and practices of media producers and consumers."[12] Or, building on James Carey's terminology, media regimes may be understood as formations that specify ritualized interactions between producers and consumers during a particular historical period. If journalism is a cultural institution, media regimes are historically contingent expressions of journalism in time.

The dynamics of media regimes can be studied with regard to their *inter*-institutional dynamics as well as their *intra*-institutional characteristics. As already indicated in the introductory chapter, institutionalists have been mostly concerned with studying how journalism related to and was shaped by other societal institutions. Their work examines how the "broader institutional environment of the public sphere provides crucial definitions of, and legitimacy for, the news organization's tasks."[13] Introducing the term *regime* in this context provided an opportunity to conceptualize how dominant political, social, and economic forces shape a particular formation of journalism. However, while institutional analysis effectively demonstrated how journalism intersects with other institutions and how a certain uniformity of journalistic practices can be explained by extraneous forces, it has not sufficiently conceptualized how journalists, editors, and other news workers influence the formation of media regimes from the bottom up. In other words, institutional analysis was more interested in the macro-meso interactions and less on the micro-meso dynamics. In doing so, it has advanced a sometimes deterministic understanding of journalism, overstating structural constraints and underestimating the agency of news workers. An *intra*-institutional perspective of studying media regimes would take a slightly different approach and focus on how institutional dynamics in journalism can be described and explained by examining the activities of news workers, news organizations, and their professional networks. This perspective informs the work of scholars who are interested in bringing the actors back in. Lowndes and Roberts describe this approach as "institutional emergence."[14] In this context, scholars examine "how groups coalesce to make claims for or against certain practices or actors in order to create or resist new institutional arrangements or transform existing ones."[15] Transposing this view to journalism means not just acknowledging exogenous forces on the formation of journalism as an institution but also the importance of endogenous factors such as the imagination, creativity, entrepreneurship, and literary sensibility of journalists. At the same time, those endogenous factors feed from and resonate with a particular cultural climate, providing the language in which action is constituted.

Building on this intra-institutional approach, my focus in this chapter is on how reporters and editors mobilized rhetorical resources to introduce, justify, and implement this alternative form of news reporting and writing. Ever since the groundbreaking newsroom ethnographies of the 1970s, journalism scholars have predominantly focused on external forces constraining the autonomy of news workers.[16] While not rejecting this approach, I here shift the lens toward the relative agency that journalists developed to shape and innovate news practices.

In this chapter, then, I trace how this emerging institutional news regime took shape between the late 1970s and late 1980s, how it was discursively constructed within newsrooms and other institutional settings, and how it became possible for such a different epistemological framework to evolve in an industry as seemingly ossified as the U.S. newspaper industry had been to that point. Before turning to the larger trade context, however, it is necessary to take a closer look at one experiment at a single newspaper that became a test case within the American Society of Newspaper Editors for promoting the value of storytelling.

The Storytelling Experiment

One of the leading figures in improving writing in an effort to win back readers was Eugene C. Patterson, who, after leaving the *Washington Post* and teaching at Duke University, had been the editor-in-chief of the *St. Petersburg (FL) Times* since 1972. He was present at the aforementioned ASNE meeting in 1976 in Honolulu and wanted his paper to become a test case for demonstrating what improved writing in a newspaper could look like. The *Times* already had a good reputation as one of the best small-city newspapers in the country, but Patterson was not satisfied with the status quo. He deemed his paper's writing "flat and uninspired."[17] In 1977, Patterson reached out to a young English professor at Auburn University at Montgomery, Alabama, about whom he heard from his executive editor Robert Haiman. That professor was Roy Peter Clark. In his recruitment letter, Patterson emphasized that improving newspaper writing was not just a goal of the *St. Petersburg Times* but also of ASNE more generally, where Patterson would be the incoming president later that year. His expectations for the young English professor were ambitious. Patterson told Clark he wanted him to "enliven the tired blood of literary hacks who quit learning when they started writing for newspapers"[18] and in another letter called him the "white hope of academe to provide the practical means of illumination by which the news business can find its way back from darkness toward literacy."[19] In the summer of 1977, Clark was hired as a writing consultant, initially for one year, and expected to work with editors and reporters at the *St. Petersburg Times*, becoming the industry's first *de facto* full-time writing coach.[20]

Patterson's recruitment of Clark highlights how unusual it was to bring an untested outsider into the newsroom and expect him or her to change ingrained writing practices and editorial routines. Not only was it unheard of to focus on writing training, there was not even much attention to provide training beyond the traditional reporter-editor relationship at all. "Perhaps the best way to teach writing," a report of the APME Writing Committee said in 1977, "is to use the old city editor's hammer, which by constant application to the head of the offender results in improvement in style and in readability of copy."[21] Journalists were expected to learn to write by trial and error, with more or less help from editors. As Robert Darnton described the process, most journalists "acquire attitudes, values, and a professional ethos while serving as copy boys in the city room; and they learn to perceive news and to communicate it while being 'broken in' as rookie reporters."[22] In addition, the profession as a whole was wary of outsiders trying to tell practicing journalists how they could improve their work. To address this potentially skeptical attitude Patterson was keen to preempt any suspicion or trepidation toward the new consultant. "Roy is an unusual kind of professor," he said in a newsletter announcing the arrival of Clark. "He can relate to newspaper people. He's able, he's young, he's fascinated by newspapers."[23]

Clark himself emphasized that he came as a curious novice and a humble student. "At least half of this year will be an educational process for me," he was quoted as saying. "I have no newspaper background at all. Before I can make any suggestions as to what the papers can do as an institution, I have to acquaint myself with deadlines."[24] Clark grew up in Long Island and studied medieval literature at the State University of New York at Stony Brook, where he received his doctorate degree. While teaching in Alabama and eager to find some distraction from academic life, Clark began writing columns for newspapers about Southern culture. In 1975, the *New York Times* published one of his pieces with the title "Infectious Cronkitis."[25] In it, Clark bemoaned the fact that "Southern newsmen have abandoned the dialect of their home-lands for the colorless, cracked-twig dialect promulgated by major networks and university broadcasting schools." In retrospect, Clark described the publication of this column as an eye-opening experience. He said he realized the power of public discourse and the possibility of writing that could be done "in the blink of an eye," unlike the tedious process of academic publishing.[26] When Patterson contacted him, Clark still thought of himself as a scholar but one who was curious about the world of newspapers. He wanted to learn more about it, mostly to be able to somehow teach about it. His plan was to go to St. Petersburg for a year and then resume his position at Auburn University.

When reporters were later asked how they had anticipated the experience of working with Clark, their answers indicated mostly reservations and distrust. "I thought back to all the college English professors I had ever had and said, 'Jesus Christ!'" one reporter remembered. "I was okay," another one said, "until I heard he didn't know anything about newspapers, had never written for a newspaper story on deadline, had never set foot in a newspaper, and then I began to wonder how could this Ph.D. possibly be able to tell me anything when he doesn't know anything about what daily newspaper writing is." A third one added, "I feared he'd be an agent of management, reporting back to [executive editor Bob] Haiman and Patterson about flaws in my writing. I thought Patterson had finally flipped a wig."[27]

These initial expectations not only indicate the cultural climate in the newsroom (as elsewhere in the industry) at the time. They also resonate with a large body of journalism research describing journalistic practice as a highly routinized activity, shaped by organizational constraints and professional frames.[28] For many reporters at the *St. Petersburg Times*, bringing in an outsider signaled a disruption of such routines, a potential threat to their journalistic self-understanding, and a challenge to the *esprit de corps* of the newspaper. The *St. Petersburg* newsroom, like other papers' during that era, reflected a common understanding of journalism as straight news reporting, reinforced by a culture of entrenched practices geared toward the ideal of objectivity. Schudson, and other scholars after him, described objectivity as an occupational norm that arose from a process of professionalization in U.S. journalism.[29] According to this ideal, reporters were supposed to be detached observers who chronicled events with dispassionate neutrality. In terms of news writing, this ideal found its expression in the inverted pyramid form: frontloading the news content at the expense of plot or narrative line. That was the environment that marked the point of departure for Clark.

To engage with reporters, Clark applied various strategies toward achieving the goal of improving writing in the newsroom. He sat down for individual consulting sessions, interviewed reporters about their writing routines, and reviewed articles, looking for strengths and weaknesses. Every week he organized a brown bag lunch and picked an example of narrative journalism that served as a prompt for a general debate about what made for good writing. Selected writings included pieces by, for example, Jimmy Breslin, Nora Ephron, Norman Mailer, and Tom Wolfe. In a weekly newsletter called *The Wind Bag*, Clark discussed the writing at the newspaper, provided examples of good writing, and reflected on general issues of news writing. Even though it was not a declared goal in these endeavors, narrative storytelling rose to the surface and was soon actively promoted as exemplary practice. Moreover, elevating writing to a topic of conversation in the newsroom created a space for stretching the boundaries of what daily journalism in the newspaper might look like. "I didn't have the language I have now to describe what I was seeing," Clark recalled as he was looking back at his experience in St. Petersburg. What he was looking for, he said, was clarity in the news reports along with interesting compelling details and the personal writing voice of reporters. "What I noticed about the newsroom," Clark remembered, was that "they were expert practitioners of a certain form of writing but they were not self-conscious and a little skeptical of theories and ideas and concepts about writing and learning, even about their own craft." Clark did not promote any particular form of storytelling or a specific concept of narrative. Instead, his goal was to teach a critical vocabulary so that reporters and editors would have a shared understanding about how to construct good stories, both as reports and narratives.

In this context, the newsletter particularly served as a platform to discuss writing more generally. And it was in this context that Clark had an opportunity to talk about how narrative techniques could be used in everyday stories. In *Wind Bag* #13, for example, Clark juxtaposes two versions of a news story—one straight news, the other narrative—and analyzes their differences. In both cases the headline reads, "Boy Trying to Save His Dog Is Hit by Train, Loses Legs." But while the first version is written using the inverted pyramid approach, the second employs a more narrative structure. For example, the first version begins with a traditional hard-news lead: "While trying to save his fuzzy, new puppy on a train trestle, a 10-year-old boy fell beneath the wheels of an Amtrak passenger train and lost both his legs below the knee." In contrast, the second version begins by setting the scene:

> The last day of their precious holiday vacation found James Harper, his dog Misty and their friend Jeff Tawzer shuffling along the graying, metal train trestle spanning the Hillsborough River.

Like Tom Sawyer and Huck Finn exploring the banks of the Big Muddy, 10-year old James, 12-year old Jeff and many other children must have mapped the paths that lace the tall grass along the river and shinnied up the tall, thick trees that flourish on its banks.

The specific information about how the boy lost his legs is only presented in the ninth paragraph: "Somehow, James slipped and his legs were caught and completely severed below the knees by the metal wheels." For Clark, this contrast "illustrate[s] some interesting problems about news writing." Apparently aware of how his in-house readers had been shaped by traditional news writing norms, he writes: "No doubt, some will be turned off by the second version. You have to read well into the story to get the hard news. And the analogy of the two wandering boys to Tom Sawyer and Huck Finn may seem gratuitous. These are valid criticisms." Following up on this introductory statement, Clark emphasizes the benefits of a narrative approach: "I find the second version more readable for a number of reasons: 1) the hard news is right there in the headline and need not be repeated in the lead; 2) the narrative approach gives the story a more coherent structure—a clearly defined beginning, middle, and end; 3) the narrative carries the reader through the story and gives him more incentive to read the *whole* thing." Framing the discussion along these lines, Clark acknowledges that a narrative approach to news writing was not necessarily a common practice during this era. But he also slowly challenged a newsroom mentality that was reluctant to embrace other forms of news writing.

Clark's arguments are illuminating because they reflect and anticipate larger debates about how to lend more legitimacy to narrative writing in daily newspaper journalism. He argued that a narrative approach did not take away from conveying information but, to the contrary, could enhance the content and experience of the story. Clark complemented his assessment with interviews of the writer and the editor of this particular story (Frank DeLoache and Steve Nohlgren, respectively). When asked about the difference in style, DeLoache explained that the first version had been written on deadline for the first edition. Then the editor suggested a rewrite. "We figured most people will have heard the story on TV," DeLoache said. "If not, when they read this headline they'll know that a boy lost his legs. So what the TV couldn't paint in pictures . . . the description of the area . . . that's what we thought we'd feature." Nohlgren, the editor, emphasized the point that there was something in the story that warranted a different treatment. He was intrigued by the description of the neighborhood and the setting and felt that there "was something that was drawing the children there and may have played [a] part in the disaster." His goal was to sustain that mood and tell the story in a narrative way. As Nohlgren said, "You can almost always re-create an event better with straight narration than you can in a more convoluted fashion often imposed by newswriting." This was an interesting insight coming from a reporter in the field, namely that now it was the traditional, inverted pyramid form that looked more convoluted whereas the story form stood for clarity.

While this example is a singular instance in one particular newspaper, it illustrates a number of important factors in the emergence of narrative journalism in the daily newspaper. Narrative writing had already been appearing elsewhere, but only at the initiative of maverick editors in specialized publications.[30] In most newspaper dailies at the time, the reporter might not have included descriptive, sensory details in the first place, and the second version might not have been produced at all if it had not been triggered by encouragement from the editor. Under Clark's prompting, now it would happen at the hands of the reporter-writer alone. Moreover, while the newsroom had accommodated itself to traditional news norms, Clark pressed it to see how the narrative approach allowed the story to carry specific pieces of information that not only set it apart from other media (television) but that also supplemented more conventional straight news reporting. As Nohlgren suggested, narrative writing may serve explanatory purposes when it points out circumstances that "may have played [a] part in the disaster." Admittedly, these explanations are more implied than stated and thus circumvent the traditional requirement of solely including information that can be attributed. But as Clark knew, the reporter is not arguing that particular circumstances explain everything; rather, his narrative approach thickens the texture of the news article, offering the reader some context for the incident. True, as Clark cautioned in his interpretation, this approach "would not work for some stories." He mentioned the recent example of a breaking news story about a particular murder case where "it would not be appropriate to write a lead that traces the girls' activities the night of the killings and to move to a point (in the middle of the story) where the girls are murdered." Nonetheless, this episode illustrates how narrative journalism necessarily introduces perspective and judgment, and thus raises the matter of explanation, interpretations that traditional newswriting eschews. In addition, narrative carries two types of explanations, implicit and explicit ones. Implicit explanations derive from narrative as a particular structure that creates coherence. Explicit explanations are folded into the plot.

As Clark put narrative writing on the agenda, he provided a frame of reference to discuss its strengths and weaknesses in a newsroom environment. Throughout his tenure as writing coach, he validated the use of narrative technique and legitimated alternative ways of doing journalism. When the *St. Petersburg Times* asked its reporters about their experiences under Clark's tutelage, the reviews were glowing. "It's been the most important thing that's ever happened to me in my four years as a pro," wrote one reporter. "He made me realize," wrote another, "that the police beat has just as many opportunities for good writing as the Sunday features or the magazine." One reporter praised the brown bag lunches as inspiring. "Just the idea of being able to sit with about 20 or other reporters for an hour and really study a piece of good origin, trying to dissect what made it distinctive, has a real effect on you. It sounds corny [. . .], but, you know, after we spend a whole hour talking at lunch about writing, we come out of that lunchroom just like the Notre Dame football team, all fired up to go back to work and really work on our writing."[31] Some staff members noticed a cultural change in the newsroom, as this comment by a young reporter indicates:

> [Clark] has raised the consciousness of the staff to good writing. In the old days if you walked around the newsroom and just listened to what people were saying, you would hear people talking about reporting problems and production problems, not about writing and editing problems. They would be talking about deadlines, about cops who were withholding information, about councilmen who were holding secret meetings, about terminals which were not working, about photo orders which got lost, about having to go early with the first editions because we had a big run and a collapsed press. But we are supposed to be writers as well as reporters, and you hardly ever heard anybody talking about writing in the city room. Now you hear people all the time talking about leads and transitions and analogies and similes and imagery and usage and symbolism and quotes and color and even poetry. In the old days one reporter might call another over to check out a fact on some history on a story which occurred before he arrived. Now you hear people asking their friends to come over to their terminal and check out the writing style of their story before they turn in a piece.[32]

This year-long initiative forged a culture of writing, created a new "interpretive community,"[33] and established rules and rituals for embedding narrative journalism in daily newspaper production. Moreover, this experiment at the *St. Petersburg Times*, far from being an isolated instance, would become an exemplary case in the newspaper industry. It was highly praised and widely advertised during subsequent ASNE conventions and in the *ASNE Bulletin*, as the next section will show.

Transforming the Industry

The *St. Petersburg* experiment came at a time when editors had begun to play a more active role in shaping the conversation about writing in newspapers. Just as Patterson's experiment was taking form, these conversations took place within the networks of ASNE and APME, at conventions, in targeted publications (*ASNE Bulletin, The Editors' Exchange, APME News*), working groups and committees (ASNE and APME), as well as in letters that circulated among the leadership. Editors at APME were already discussing issues such as a general appreciation of writing (writing matters), basics and mechanics (clarity, precision, correct usage), as well as complex ideas (good writing comes from good reporting; narrative writing). Taken together, these conversations would elevate narrative techniques from a niche in the spectrum of journalistic writing and construct narrative journalism as a legitimate practice.

ASNE and APME had different but overlapping constituencies among executive editors at newspapers. ASNE was more selective and focused on big, contemporary issues of journalism, also offering a stage to cabinet officials, the president, and visiting heads of state. Its members were the "Brahmins of the newspaper industry," and former *Washington Post* editor Russell Wiggins characterized ASNE as "an organization which, if any more loosely organized, would fall apart, and if any more closely organized would be a menace."[34] The formal writing improvement program at ASNE coincided with the organization's desire to become a more powerful player in the newspaper industry generally. After years of having been "too loosely structured" and "too narrowly focused," ASNE wanted to "become a really major policymaking force in the council of publishers."[35] The organization actively lobbied for a seat at the table of the newly founded Newspaper Readership Project, an initiative in association with the National Advertising Bureau and the American Newspaper Publishers Association to increase the readership of newspapers.

APME had started out in the 1930s with a narrow focus to critique AP news reports and then bring that critique to AP executives. Over time, however, that effort "broadened into a much wider range of professional interests—pushing for better writing and pictures, encouraging higher ethical standards, better newsroom management, more professional hiring and promotion practices, more competent editing and opening opportunities for women and minorities."[36] At the core of APME's work were the more than a dozen continuing study committees. While some of them were specifically tasked with providing feedback to the AP, others strove to offer practical, hands-on information for editors. The APME Writing Committee had been in place since 1951, yet mostly examined AP copy for examples of good and bad writing, often producing bulletins with specific writing tips for news writers. These activities gave little attention to systematic analysis or deeper reflection about the opportunities and constraints of newspaper writing. As late as 1977, the writing committee stated that, "There is no royal road to good writing, as there isn't to geometry."[37]

Triggered by ASNE's announcement of the writing improvement program, however, conversations about writing gained momentum in the late 1970s and often played out in the *ASNE Bulletin*. "Until the past decade or so, only a few daily newspapers in this country regularly blessed good writing," wrote James Ragdale in 1979. "In fact, over the years some of the best writing has appeared in weekly newspapers. Now, more and more editors are learning what good writers have known all along: Good readers need good writers."[38] Such conversations, in time, created a public forum for reflecting not only on the nuts and bolts of technique but also on the purpose and possibilities of alternatives to traditional news writing. Editors, for example, now had an opportunity to formulate how they envisioned the successful combination of reporting and writing. As some editors argued, the best writing was not merely clear and concise but added a certain sparkle. For Claude Sitton, of *The News & Observer* and *The Raleigh Times*, the best newspaper writing "captures the essence of the subject in a concise and interesting manner and that [. . .] *reflects exceptional imagination in construction and approach* to the subject." When Jim Hoge of the *Chicago Sun-Times/ Daily News* was asked what he would like to see recognized in a potential writing award, he responded that they "should *reflect the emotional and intellectual range of journalism. We enlighten, provoke and entertain.*"[39] Both statements would seem to offer rather general definitions that may apply to a variety of different styles. But by connecting good writing with imagination, and emphasizing the intellectual and emotional range of journalism, these quotes illustrate how narrative journalism was implicitly featured and even endorsed, expanding journalism's boundaries beyond routinized, formulaic news writing.

The ferment of improving writing in the field of newspapers was particularly visible during the annual ASNE conference in 1978, where Patterson served as the incoming president of the organization. In that position he would succeed a handful of predecessors who had already reformed and transformed ASNE by strengthening study committees, improving the *Bulletin*, and elevating the organization's stature.[40] Under Patterson, however, ASNE also joined the Readership Project, "an unprecedented cooperative attempt by the American newspaper industry to halt the downward trend in newspaper readership and circulation."[41] The conference offered a stage for Patterson to advertise the *St. Petersburg* experiment to editors from around the country and allowed him to stake out his personal philosophy. In his president's report, Patterson set the tone and sketched an agenda for expanding editors' role in defining the place of journalism in the changing media environment of the late 1970s. He argued that journalism had developed from the "obedient press" in the 1950s toward "adversary journalism" in the 1960s and 1970s. The latter made for "a sturdier press and a stronger society." Yet, Patterson warned that "throwing rocks at authority is not enough" and suggested some kind of "better reporting of issues" as the way forward, calling this approach explanatory journalism. He primarily had public affairs reporting in mind, encouraging reporters to "commit to the goal of telling an issue whole—taking greater responsibility for bringing clarity to the pros and cons of it." Nevertheless, he added that this clarity derives from "*simplicity which can only spring from a writer's comprehension*." Patterson was not only implying that proficient writing produces better comprehension by making complex issues more accessible. Importantly, he was also arguing that the reporter was more than a human recording device, someone who brought intelligence and comprehension (i.e., subjectivity) to an understanding of the story. In his institutional role as leader of the industry, Patterson was suggesting that a better grasp of both content and form made for better journalism insofar as it allowed readers to "more clearly comprehend the issues." Patterson's idea of explanatory journalism did not propose a specific form of writing. But it was clear that with his call for explanatory journalism, Patterson opened the gates for narrative journalism as one form of explaining complex issues.[42]

Writing and the improvement of writing also took center stage at a panel titled "Can Writing Be Taught?," which provided a platform for Roy Peter

Clark to personally interact with the assembled ASNE community for the first time. As during his time in the newsroom, Clark emphasized that good writing was a result of both mastering the practice and creating an environment that valued the written word. Clark took editors on a *tour d'horizon* of what better writing in newspapers could look like. He described his activities at the *St. Petersburg Times* (*The Wind Bag*, weekly lunches) and offered specific tips and guidelines for implementing similar initiatives in newsrooms. He concluded his presentation by establishing a direct connection between core journalistic values and the importance of clear, precise, and imaginative journalistic writing. "Good writing may help you sell newspapers," he said, "but good writing also has important political implications for a democracy. [...] On the top of the editorial page of the *St. Petersburg Times* is a quotation from Paul Poynter, publisher of the paper from 1912 to 1950: 'The policy of our paper is very simple—merely to tell the truth.' Let us all tell the truth and tell it well."[43] This rhetorical move connects good writing with the self-image of journalists as bearers of the democratic torch and argues that the core mission of journalism can only be carried out when attuned to the specifics of language. With these words, Clark made the case that writing was not something decorative outside the purview of journalism but part of its substance. In addition, however, Clark's rhetoric also illustrates how narrative techniques were becoming part of mainstream journalism, the same techniques that some of the New Journalists and their proponents characterized as rebellious.

Clark's presentation and the *St. Petersburg* experience sparked interest for launching writing initiatives and spurred experimentation in newsrooms across the country, as numerous articles in trade journals, journalism reviews, and other correspondence between editors document. After the 1978 conference, more than 1,500 copies of a special report on writing that Clark had produced were distributed by the ASNE secretary to editors and reporters.[44] Within the next three years, Clark would give fifty seminars in twenty-seven states, with most interest from papers whose circulation ranged from 15,000 to 75,000.[45] At the same time, narrative journalists had been actively involved in efforts to explain and create awareness for their narrative approach to news. They were seizing opportunities to demonstrate how they were rethinking and reimagining daily reporting and writing techniques. And it was ASNE that provided them a stage. In 1978 ASNE had begun organizing annual contests to identify and reward excellent writing in American newspapers. It was an attempt to emphasize that there were already best practices and news writers that could serve as examples. The award committee consisted of editors from major newspapers and reflected geographic variety.[46] The award ceremony became an integral part of ASNE's annual conventions. The prizes were awarded during the conference banquet and beginning in 1980, award winners were invited to join a panel discussion and talk about their writing. Then the award-winning stories were published by the newly established Modern Media Institute (later Poynter Institute) as a series called *Best Newspaper Writing*. The anthology was published from 1979 until 2008. In the first few years, Clark edited the book, interviewed the reporters, and provided notes and comments.

The *Best Newspaper Writing* anthologies not only showcased the best writing in newspapers but also contained interviews with the award-winning journalists. Just like oral history interviews, these conversations capture the subjectivity of experiences as they not only describe what reporters did but also "what they wanted to do, what they believed they were doing, what they [. . .] think they did."[47] An important motivation for practicing narrative journalism and implementing it in daily newspaper production was journalists' desire to humanize the news. They were interested in telling stories about people and how they lived their lives. They wanted to explore the emotional core of how events and experiences affected people in their attitudes and their behavior. Their goal was to engage readers not only with reports that informed their minds but with stories that touched their hearts.[48]

Newsrooms, meanwhile, began initiating their own writing improvement efforts. *The New York News*, for example, launched a newsletter called *The Printer's Devil* in December of 1978. Its aim was to heighten awareness of the need for good writing.[49] The *Nashville Banner* set up a writing program that included individual sessions with reporters to discuss their writing habits and technique.[50] The *Orlando Sentinel Star* appointed its best writer to be the main editor on the features desk and serve as a writing coach.[51] David Wood, an English professor at Augsburg College, was hired by the *Minneapolis Tribune* to join the newsroom as writing coach for one year.[52] The *Boston Globe*—which had hired Donald Murray, a professor at the University of New Hampshire, as a temporary writing coach—decided to name columnist Alan Richman an assistant manager for writing.[53] As newspapers organized writing seminars, internal workshops, and in-house critiques in all parts of the country, these efforts were widely shared and promoted in the APME writing committee and the *Editors' Exchange* newsletter.[54] Regional conferences across the country emphasized the importance of creating an atmosphere that was sensitive to writing.[55] In 1980, two years after his original presentation to ASNE editors, Clark presented further evidence that writing initiatives in individual newsrooms had expanded.[56] And he looked optimistically into the future.

> I foresee a great time ahead for newspaper writing. We have purged ourselves of the abuses of the New Journalism—the self-indulgent overwriting, the composite characters, the interior monologues. But we have absorbed into everyday news reporting many of the techniques of that movement: setting scenes, using perspective, letting characters speak, using significant detail.[57]

To some, however, Clark's prognosis might have seemed premature. Especially when the tension between narrative journalism's possibilities and its potential pitfalls became a central issue with the Janet Cooke scandal in 1981.

Narrative Journalism and Its Discontents

There was no bigger challenge to narrative writing in newspapers in the 1980s than the Janet Cooke scandal. When the *Washington Post* had to forfeit a Pulitzer Prize in feature writing because it was discovered that its reporter Janet Cooke had fabricated the story of an eight-year-old heroin addict in Washington, DC, the ensuing debates provided a platform for the journalistic community to discuss the merits and flaws of narrative techniques.[58] On the surface, the scandal was about anonymous sources, confidentiality, and the relationship between reporters and editors, as well as the complicated and precarious status of black reporters in American newsrooms. At the same time, it also reflected the newspaper industry's coming to terms with changes in reporting routines and writing conventions.[59] While the debates around Cooke's "Jimmy's World" were not exclusively about narrative technique, they did involve disagreements about narrative storytelling and the legacy of the New Journalism. Even though there was widespread consensus that lying and inventing characters were egregious transgressions, some journalists and editors used the scandal to put narrative journalism on trial. Examining these debates illustrates the continuing conflicted attitudes and approaches to narrative storytelling in newspapers. It became, in other words, an exemplary case of boundary work, a collective effort to identify "good" journalism, purge inappropriate or unethical practices, and thereby renew journalistic authority. The scandal triggered widespread and diverse responses from other newspapers and media organizations, often focusing on the admissibility of anonymous sources and the boundaries of confidentiality.

But it was not *only* about authority. The Jimmy story also had all the ingredients of a powerful piece of narrative journalism: a compelling character (an eight-year-old addict), scene setting (the "ghetto" in southeast Washington, DC), descriptive details and vivid images ("The needle slides into the boy's soft skin like a straw pushed into the center of a freshly baked cake"), dialogue, a social issue of great importance (heroin), news value (information about a new strain of heroin), and expert witnesses (DEA officer, medical experts, social workers). While most readers probably reacted to the content of the story, some also noticed the particular form of the article and their immediate reaction to the narrative form was mixed. For reader Martha S. Stewart, for example, the story "was descriptive reportage at its best."[60] In contrast, Sharron Jackson expressed outrage that "the article was written as if it were a story about an 8-year-old's day in the park."[61]

Meanwhile, two of the *Post*'s major competitors on the national level also framed the scandal in terms of the uses and risks of narrative journalism. For the *Wall Street Journal*, the scandal raised "some broader and troublesome issues," including the question "Are the competitive pressures of big-city newsrooms such that style and form are overtaking substance?"[62] And Jonathan Friendly of the *New York Times* wrote:

> Many reporters and editors criticized what has come to be called the "new journalism," in which the writer presents as emotionally true composite characters who do not exist, vivid scenes he never saw and bright conversations he never heard. They said they were worried that the cachet such writing had been given would lead younger reporters in particular into trying to present it as actual reportage.[63]

Since these two interpretations synthesized and analyzed several interviews with editors and journalists, they indicated the industry's discomfort with narrative techniques in daily news journalism and reflected a deep-seated suspicion that narrative style could never be reconciled with journalistic substance. The *Post* in particular was blamed by some for having pushed too hard toward narrative writing. "I contend that *The Post*'s overheated striving for 'style' in news reporting left the newspaper wide open to being deceived as it was," wrote Don Porter, DC bureau chief of King Broadcasting, in a letter to the editor.[64]

What complicated this public reckoning, however, was the lack of a commonly accepted term for what Cooke had been doing. Many observers and commentators associated Cooke's practice with the New Journalism, defined as storytelling that may include literary license. According to this view, Cooke's transgression was not just an individual aberration but a problematic pattern that warranted closer scrutiny. Critics associated narrative techniques with *fictional* storytelling, understood as something that was invented, instead of storytelling *like* in *fiction*, understood as employing particular tools and structural techniques such as character, dialogue, and plot. Critics of narrative practices misleadingly conflated some of the New Journalism's practices—inventions, composite characters, literary license—with virtually any kind of narrative writing by journalists. Thus, the New Journalism had become a foil used to banish everything that was supposedly undermining traditional journalism. What these critics overlooked was that the New Journalism equally emphasized thorough reporting, immersion in a subject's world, and an appreciation of all things human. It was not just literary writing and its alleged blurring of fact and fiction that caused consternation but, more generally, the shift toward analytical and explanatory journalism. An editorial in the *Washington Star* diagnosed that "newspapers began to fear that the old who-what-where-when formula wasn't quite measuring up and began experimenting with 'news analysis' and 'background' stories, calling upon reporters not merely to report the 'facts' but to place them in context and perspective. Raw information was to be augmented by meaning."[65]

Yet, for some commentators the emergence of narrative journalism was not a bad development at all. The *Columbia Journalism Review*, while pointing out the Cooke scandal was a "cautionary tale about a significant change that has been taking place in the way newspaper reporters and editors see their jobs," provided a succinct appreciation of narrative journalism's impact:

> For twenty years or so, reporters on the *Washington Post* and other newspapers have been at pains to go beyond the chronicling of daily happenings on clearly defined beats, and to report on how groups of people—women, blacks, migrant workers, singles in suburbia, illegal Mexican immigrants, residents of particular neighborhoods—live, and how they feel about their lives. Journalists have become anthropologists, and works of anthropology are held up as models for students at journalism schools. The results have often been impressive. Indeed, there should be more reporting of this kind [. . .].[66]

The Cooke scandal provided an occasion and served as a catalyst to discuss broader changes in journalism and their implications for daily practice in newspapers. But as one observer noticed, while this debate was fruitful in clarifying narrative techniques and their value in daily news reporting, there was also a danger "that guilt by association would be invoked to undercut the long-standing struggle to make newspapers readable."[67] That the Cooke scandal posed a serious threat to the efforts of ASNE editors to improve newspaper writing was illustrated in a follow-up piece to the scandal that included a reference to another case of fabrication at the *New York Daily News*:

> The Washington and New York incidents have led some editors to reexamine the decade-long emphasis they have placed on "good writing." Eager to present lively articles that compete successfully with television for reader attention, many editors checked the clippings of job applicants with more of an eye for the well-turned phrase than the well-gathered fact.[68]

The expansion of narrative journalism might have just stopped here. After all, if the demands of narrativity had not been able to meet the test of reality, they might not have been a good fit for journalism to begin with.

Humanizing the News

After the Cooke scandal, adopting narrative techniques in daily news production was being contested within the industry. While certain editors actively promoted new formats, styles, and content—often looking to magazines for inspiration—others perceived these changes as a turn toward "last-gasp 'daily magazines'" and instead advocated for "a hard line for hard news."[69] Moreover, some editors and observers had the uneasy feeling that narrative writing signified a triumph of style over substance, a turn toward "soft and sexy" and the danger that reporters "will spend more time searching for flashy metaphors and dramatic stories than for verifiable facts and legitimate news."[70] Clark himself addressed these criticisms by implicitly invoking the Cooke scandal. In the introduction to the 1982 anthology of *Best Newspaper Writing*, he wrote, "In an era of Pulitzer hoaxes and recycled advice columns it needs to be said—though it should be obvious—that we do not stand for dishonest writing. Dishonest writing is bad writing, no matter how beautiful the style, for it perverts clear communication and violates the trust that bonds the writer and the reader."[71] Clark took advantage of his then new role as associate director of the Modern Media Institute and invoked the existence of a "writing movement" that stood "for clarity, relevance, humanity, hard work and the right work in the right place." Its proponents, he argued, "believe that strong reporting makes good writing possible."[72]

But how enduring were the efforts of Patterson, Clark, the ASNE and its advocates of narrative journalism in the newsroom? How lasting were the notions of being able to humanize the news, and to engage readers at an emotional level that connected to their daily lives? How radical a change had this been, and how much of a setback had the Cooke scandal—the first of many, alas—really been? To answer that question, we should turn to the memories and testimonies of reporters (and some editors) themselves, who were, in this era, trying to make sense of their routines and how they positioned themselves vis-à-vis traditional practices of straight news reporting. We need to learn how, especially when outlining practices of narrative reporting and writing, these journalists formulated shared practices and formed a body of knowledge, discursively constructing an emerging framework of norms, values, and beliefs with respect to narrative journalism.[73]

From the perspective of many writers and editors, it turns out, narrative writing still provided efficient tools to write about big events and trends (i.e., disasters, the "mood" in a particular community, events of national interest, foreign news) as well as personal, intimate experiences. Thomas Oliphant, who won the ASNE news/nondeadline category in 1979 with a story that reconstructed how the Boston area had been hit by a major blizzard, considered narrative as the "best way to reconstruct major events." In his view, "newspapers don't do enough of it."[74] While Oliphant was specifically talking about narrative journalism, this label was not widely used by reporters and editors. Instead, individual newsrooms came up with their own names and called these stories that explored larger trends or specific contexts "a read" (*Philadelphia Inquirer*), "sweep pieces" (*Los Angeles Herald Examiner*), or characterized their approach to in-depth, narrative stories as "more typical of a national magazine approach than a newspaper approach" (*Boston Globe*).[75]

These journalists emphasized the importance of reporting, but they also underscored that their reporting differed from standard news reporting. "It's the reporting that underlies the good writing," said Carol McCabe, who won the award in the news category in 1980 for her environmental reporting. "You've got to have the basic facts to build on, and you work with language in a way that makes it not 'fancier'—I like 'plainer.'"[76] For Cynthia Gorney, then the West Coast reporter for the *Washington Post* Style section, reporting narrative stories often included "mucking around in people's tragedies" and the challenge was "not to go crazy with grief but at the same time respond the way a human being ought to respond." She won the features award in 1980 for a series of stories, one of which was a profile of Sirhan Sirhan, the murderer of Robert F. Kennedy. When describing her reporting style, she indicated that it sometimes clashed with traditional notions of journalistic detachment. "I cry a lot on stories. The first time it happened I thought, Now what kind of reporter are you? You're supposed to be tough and aloof."[77] What Gorney was struggling with, it seems, was that emotional involvement typically disqualified professional reporters. Yet, as she and others were discovering, in the process of reporting narrative stories, allowing emotions was not only crucial for establishing trust with sources but also for gaining insights.[78]

Several reporters mentioned that traditional fact-gathering techniques were not sufficient for narrative writing, acknowledging that the emotional content of newsgathering had specific consequences for writing such stories. "The whole idea is feeling with the protagonist or network of people in your story," said Joe Nawrozski of the *News American* in Baltimore. "It's OK to feel. If you don't feel, here comes the inverted pyramid again. [. . .] I'm not ashamed to say that I feel some empathy with the people I write about."[79] This different way of reporting posed some practical challenges for reporters' journalistic self-image and required them to negotiate professional values such as objectivity. "I believe that there is not as much objectivity possible in journalism as some observers feel, because as long as you have human beings selecting facts that are used, it comes through a subjective mind," said McCabe of the *Providence Sunday Journal*. "A reporter expressing his feelings should never replace the plain statement of fact, but I think we need people who will go and try to explain what is beyond those facts."[80]

This critical stance toward the notion of objectivity—while simultaneously emphasizing emotionality and empathy—was reflected in various interviews. But far from embracing subjectivity as merely a self-centered and solipsistic perspective instead, many narrative writers indicated how making personal judgments necessarily implies uncertainty. As Saul Pett of the Associated Press explained his approach to "mood pieces"—stories that aim to capture a community's atmosphere, "It's unscientific. I don't attempt a poll or anything. I do talk to people. The man in the street. I also talk to people in a position to catch the mood in the community. Observers and people watchers." (Pett won the 1981 award for nondeadline writing with a piece that reflected on the national mood by portraying Asheville, North Carolina.)

"How do I know I'm going to be accurate about suggesting a general mood?" he said. "Well, again, after a while you get a sameness. You begin to hear the same things over and over again. That's when you begin to get confident."[81] While acknowledging imperfection and ambivalence about personal judgments, narrative journalists expressed confidence about making them. "In every story, there are certain conclusions that any prudent man could draw from a set of facts or observations," said William Blundell, who would later write the influential book *The Art and Craft of Feature Writing*.[82]

For many writers, narrative journalism provided a method to combine the emotional content of a story with the requirements for news and information. They found inspiration in fiction writing and then adapted literary techniques to weave news into the narrative. Richard Zahler said that the "experience of literature" helped him to find a balance between information and emotion. "I'm a strong believer in story telling as story telling," he said. "The thing has got to move and develop. It's got to have detail and real people and feeling and emotion."[83] Likewise, many of these journalists expressed that the traditional formulas for news writing, such as the inverted pyramid, were only of limited use. The inverted pyramid is "an outline, it's easy to do, and in a lot of cases it fills the need," said Joe Nawrozski. "But if you have an opportunity to get deeper, to add some feeling to a breaking story, it's so much stronger. It's also much more informative and entertaining."[84]

The challenge, as many of the narrative journalists saw it, was finding the small story that illuminated the larger, the microcosm that encapsulated the macrocosm, the personal story that held universal appeal. "The goal is not to experience a particular session of the legislature or a particular house fire, but to find the things that really affect the world one way or another, things which make a difference, and try to come to some understanding of what is going on and try to explain it in a way that is accessible to people," said Peter Rinearson of the *Seattle Times*, who won an ASNE award for business writing and a Pulitzer for his story about the making of the Boeing 757.[85] "The hard thing is to take that one image or example and broaden it, to try to explain in a paragraph or two how this relates to the larger story," said David Zucchino, who won the award for deadline writing in 1984. "It helps if your example is dramatic, but you have to explain how these large, historical events are focusing on one person or one place. You can broaden that into a way of showing what this is all about by giving some of the reasons, some of the causes, some of the effects."[86]

Taken together, these testimonies suggest that journalists in the early 1980s actively constructed rationales for narrative writing and thus redefined their practices for reporting and writing news stories. These journalists articulated how narrative journalism offered opportunities to combine interpretive and explanatory elements with literary techniques and emotional engagement, establishing a news culture that challenged traditional concepts of objectivity and detachment. They promoted a form of journalism that, as they perceived it, was more assertive, more creative, and more imaginative than traditional news reporting. At the same time, they emphasized the need for thorough reporting, distancing themselves from techniques that fictionalized true stories. Following the first volume in 1979, the annual editions of *Best Newspaper Writing* would become a reference text, a taxonomy of best practices, a tool to promote the growth of an interpretive community. Eventually, award-winning journalists would publish their own takes on narrative writing techniques, launching a cottage industry of books for narrative journalists.[87] An emphasis on the emotional aspect of news stories was a recurring theme as journalists discursively constructed the practice of narrative journalism. For many narrative journalists, something had been lacking in traditional news accounts, and that was the emotional, the human side of news. This was not "human interest" journalism in the traditional sense as it evolved in the late nineteenth century, "chatty little reports of tragic or comic incidents in the lives of people."[88] Rather this kind of discursive construction subverted the distinction between information and human interest, demonstrating that informative content could be focused on people, both as sources and as readers. It also demonstrated that supposedly soft journalism relied as much on hard facts as traditional news reporting.

Narrative journalism is often conflated with tabloidization and sensationalism, maybe because both share an interest in the emotional side of news.[89] However, the difference between narrative journalism and sensationalism is one of purpose. Sensationalism aims at provoking strong emotional responses merely for effect. Narrative journalism aims at creating emotional involvement to provide a fuller picture of the human experience. Sensationalism is instrumentalizing narrative tools; narrative journalism is adopting them to enhance the experience of learning about the world. When reporters and editors advocated for narrative strategies, as the previous section has shown, they emphasized the qualities of analytical and interpretive tools to capture aspects of the news that traditional journalism failed to grasp. At the same time, they anchored their narrative approaches in a culture of reporting, fact-checking, and journalistic integrity. They wanted to humanize the news, and for many of them that meant emphasizing the emotional components of the human experience. Nevertheless, they were trying to find a balance between eliciting emotional responses from their readers and conveying information. Narrative journalism, with its use of literary techniques, provided reporters with effective tools to capture the more emotional side of news.[90]

The discursive construction of narrative journalism as a legitimate practice of newspaper writing was not limited to award-winning journalists. They were but the most visible proponents of pushing the boundaries. Over time, newsrooms across the country developed their own strategies for creating organizational cultures that embraced and propelled narrative techniques in daily news writing. In 1988, the APME Writing and Editing Committee took an in-depth look at six newsrooms that were deemed positive examples for producing well-written papers to determine "how good writing is achieved." Members of the committee went to the *Concord Monitor*, the *Philadelphia Inquirer*, the *Sacramento Bee*, the *Lexington Herald-Leader*, the *Northeast Mississippi Daily Journal*, and the *Herald* in Everett, Washington. Summarizing the results in the introduction to the report, Reid MacCluggage concluded that "good writing more often takes place in newsrooms: Where the atmosphere is relaxed. Where there is a collaborative effort between editors and reporters. And where there is risk-taking without penalties for failure."[91] This report, however, is more than an indicator of how newsrooms implemented strategies for writing improvement. It also encapsulates what leading editors on the committee considered as best practices in the industry, and how these practices had taken root in the respective newsrooms. In particular, the report highlights how thoroughly narrative writing now seemed to be at home in newsrooms across the country. These examples, then, offer illuminating insights into the motivations and the thinking of editors and journalists as they were strategically adopting narrative techniques in daily newspaper production. They also demonstrate that the implementation of narrative writing required both a consistent editorial philosophy and resources to sustain these efforts.

Out of the six papers, the *Philadelphia Inquirer* was probably the most obvious example of a respected writer's paper. It had been featured numerous times in the *ASNE Bulletin*. For instance, in October 1979 the *Bulletin* gave ample space to Steven Lovelady, then the associate editor of the *Inquirer*, to deconstruct the story structure and especially the lede of an award-winning story about the Three Mile Island nuclear disaster. He made the case that good writing further enhances a well-reported story. "Nobody expects to find a book, or a book-length article, in his friendly morning newspaper," wrote Lovelady. "So when you offer one, it had better be so compellingly written that it overcomes the inherent resistance of the reader."[92] The newsroom culture at the *Inquirer* had been formed by Eugene L. Roberts, who became executive editor in the mid-1970s and told his editors to encourage good writing. In the APME report, editors and reporters explained their formula in the following way: The *Inquirer* hired writers based on impressive clips, put good writing on page one, did not have writing coaches but "encouraged its editors to push their writers to try something different," held informal writing workshops, encouraged staff to attend industry workshops, and fostered a positive attitude among editors and writers. Narrative writing was deemed an important element of the *Inquirer*'s appeal. "As the distance from hard news increases," the report noted, "*Inquirer* writing styles become more varied, and what might be called 'literary' devices are frequently used to good effect."[93] At the *Sacramento Bee*, the driving force behind emphasizing the importance of storytelling had been editor Gregory Favre. Similar to the innovations at the *Inquirer*, the front page of the *Bee* had been opened to narrative stories if the writing was compelling. The APME report quoted one assignment editor explaining the change as follows: "Basically I tell reporters to tell me a story, spin me a tale, paint me a portrait. If you've got people, color, pathos, then that's a story that's going to compel people to read it. That's how a B-3 story becomes Page One."[94] The *Concord Monitor* followed a full-fledged strategy to break with news-writing conventions such as the inverted pyramid. "We push writers to be interpretive," editor Mike Pride was quoted as saying in the report. "Not advocacy, but being a synthesizer, using powers of observation, and bringing the past to bear. We encourage a narrative style."[95] The report included Pride's recommendations to young reporters who wanted to develop narrative writing skills. Among the work of writers such as John McPhee and Anthony Lukas, Pride mentioned Tom Wolfe's introduction to *The New Journalism* and said, "Some of it is donkeypoo, but it is a good discussion of making a picture of the whole by describing in detail the parts. (What Wolfe calls status detail.)"[96] Pride would serve as administrator of the Pulitzer Prizes from 2014 to 2017.

Allocating resources was a crucial component in all six newsrooms. At the *Lexington Herald-Leader*, editors organized brown bag lunches and encouraged a format that facilitated discussions between editors and writers. At the *Inquirer*, journalists benefited from internal writing workshops and access to training at industry events. Building expertise within a newsroom environment that actively rewarded outstanding writing was pursued in a similar way at the *Sacramento Bee*. Editor Gregory Favre summed up his commitment to good writing, including "recruiting dozens of reporters with strong writing skills; [. . .] undertaking ambitious special projects that free reporters for extensive research and writing; [. . .] keeping editors closely involved with reporters' projects by letting reporters' writing styles emerge without undue restraint."[97] For smaller papers like the *Herald* (Everett, Washington) and the *Northeast Mississippi Daily Journal*, the input of writing coaches was particularly important. At the *Herald*, management spent $4,000, roughly the newsroom's training budget, to bring Poynter Institute writing coach Don Fry to Everett. As a result, the lifestyle section won four consecutive first-, second-, or third-place prizes in the Penney-Missouri Journalism Awards. The *Northeast Mississippi Daily Journal* also credited Fry for improving the writing at the paper. "The seminars and writing coaches have been a source of great pride for the paper," said one editor. "Reporters and editors listen to the 'experts,' then use what they have learned." One reporter was quoted saying, "After Don Fry was here we put out some of our best papers."[98]

These experiences and how they were showcased in the APME report suggest some general observations about the state of narrative writing circa 1988. Narrative journalism was actively practiced and promoted in newspapers of different sizes. Editors and journalists were drawing from classic examples of the New Journalism but adapted it to the specific context of a daily newspaper. The adoption of narrative writing was driven by an editorial philosophy that formulated a vision, provided resources, and offered incentives. In doing so, editors and reporters discursively constructed narrative journalism not only by mobilizing rhetorical resources but also material ones, in other words, training programs, writing coaches, and cash prizes. Editors and reporters legitimated narrative writing as an approach to connect with readers and offer them compelling storytelling. Taken together, these different developments indicate that institutional change had happened and that narrative journalism had arrived in mainstream newspaper journalism.

Conclusion

As early as 1983, David Laventhol, who served as the chairman of the ASNE award judges, declared that the writing initiative was working. He said, "The range and breadth of good writing, from what we have seen on the judging committee, is nationwide; it's not confined to big newspapers or city newspapers or any region."[99] Throughout the 1980s, practices and experiments in

newsrooms across the country were routinely shared in newsletters.[100] Roy
Peter Clark had now developed a reputation as the "foremost expert"[101] in
good newspaper writing and "the dean of writing coaches."[102] The Modern
Media Institute became the Poynter Institute and systematically promoted
the practice of narrative writing by offering weekly seminars and training
materials. And by the end of the 1980s, attitudes toward improving writing
in newspapers had shifted. In 1981, when the APME Writing and Editing
Committee surveyed editors on the subject of writing, only about 10 percent
of them responded that their papers had some kind of formal writing program that included any or all of the following elements: "writing and editing
coaches, paying for writing courses, daily monitoring of less-talented writers, in-house seminars, guest speakers, daily critiques, or all of the above."[103]
In 1984, the writing committee found that 37.5 percent of the surveyed editors said their papers had started a writing improvement program.[104] And
by 1987, an overwhelming majority of editors and reporters, polls suggested,
supported the use of newsletters and other forms of in-house critique. When
asked whether these tools effectively addressed problems and successes in
reporting and writing, nine out of ten editors and seven out of ten reporters
agreed. When presented with the statement, "Because of our in-house critique, our newsroom has improved its overall performance in reporting and
writing," roughly two-thirds of editors and about half of reporters agreed.
The question was no longer, "Do newspapers need narrative writing?" but
"How can narrative writing be done in newspapers in the best possible way?"
At the same time, however, by the late 1980s the improvement of writing and
the practice of narrative writing had been decoupled from debates about the
readership woes. As the beginning of the next chapter will show in more
detail, the downward spiral of relative readership loss continued.

An emphasis on the emotional aspects of news stories was a recurring
theme as journalists discursively constructed the practice of narrative journalism. In her research on Pulitzer award–winning news stories, Karin
Wahl-Jorgensen detected a "strategic ritual of emotionality," in other words,
"an institutionalized and systematic practice of journalists narrating and infusing their reporting with emotion."[105] In doing so, Wahl-Jorgensen argued,
"journalists rely on outsourcing of emotional labor to non-journalists—the
story protagonists who are (a) authorized to express emotions in public, and
(b) whose emotions journalists can authoritatively describe without impli-
cating themselves."[106] My interpretation both supports and challenges Wahl-
Jorgensen's assessment. Narrative journalism, I would argue, provided the

very tools for "an institutionalized and systematic practice of journalists nar-rating and infusing their reporting with emotion" in that it allowed report-ers to blend interpretive and explanatory elements with literary techniques and emotional engagement. However, while the expression of emotions was "heavily policed and disciplined" in many areas of news production, narra-tive journalism subverted this logic because it actively encouraged journal-ists to become personally and emotionally involved in the reporting process, in the sense that they had enhanced their reporting by building trust, show-ing empathy, and being mindful of sensory and emotional details. Actually, as examples from award-winning journalists above demonstrate, reporters embraced this emotional involvement. For many of them, emotional in-volvement and emotional expression were intertwined through the practice of narrative reporting and writing.

For some readers, the idea of narrative journalism constituting a new and different epistemology might be puzzling. Is this not the continuation of journalism with different means?, one might wonder. Yet, the narrative form requires both a different form of exploring and a different form of knowing compared to traditional journalism. Narrative, by definition and in prac-tice, introduces perspective and judgment, both of which facilitate matters of explanation. At the same time, storytelling is intricately linked to emo-tional experience, as narratologists have demonstrated. For example, David Herman emphasizes that narrative is characterized by "a structured time-course" and a "disruption or disequilibrium" which together convey "what it's like to live through that disruption, that is, the 'qualia' (or felt, subjective awareness) of real or imagined consciousness undergoing the disruptive ex-perience."[107] Still, it is also important to emphasize that this epistemology is neither better nor worse than other forms of journalistic practice.

This chapter has shown how narrative journalism was providing a tem-plate to approach daily news writing in a more interpretive way, reconciling explanatory elements with emotional storytelling. Narrative journalism over time evolved into a distinct news regime, challenging the "strategic ritual of objectivity" by offering new forms of storytelling and methods of news gath-ering. As a regime, narrative journalism might not have toppled the "high modernism of American journalism," but it certainly transformed journalis-tic formats into a "high realism," thus augmenting the ideal of objectivity by incorporating a wider range of reporting and writing tools. Literary journal-ism, as John Pauly argued, challenged both journalism's "empire of facts" as well as literature's "garden of imagination."[108] As a consequence, storytelling in newspapers advanced an understanding of news that, while not breaking with the occupational norm of objectivity, pushed it toward incorporating more dimensions, encompassing a wider spectrum and depth of the human experience.

CHAPTER FOUR

The Movement Coalesces

The Marketplace, the Academy, and the Community of Practice

JAMES K. BATTEN was a man with courtly manners and a gentle accent from his native Virginia. While for some that summoned the image of a small-town newspaper editor, he actually ran the country's second-largest newspaper chain, Knight-Ridder, which included the *Miami Herald*, the *Philadelphia Inquirer*, the *Detroit Free Press*, and the *San Jose Mercury News*.[1] As the 1980s were coming to an end, he had a strong message for the newspaper industry: "The days when we could do newspapering our way, and tell the world to go to hell if it didn't like the results, are gone."[2] Instead, he argued, journalists and editors would need to connect with their readers if they wanted to succeed in the 1990s. To illustrate his point, Batten contrasted his former belief that newspapers should mainly aspire to earn readers' respect with his new conviction that newspapers should cultivate their affection. Respect was indispensable, he said, but also cold and devoid of emotional attachment, potentially failing to truly connect readers to their newspapers. Batten then advocated for a more holistic appeal for newspapers, including the need to elicit affection. "I want them to be warm and caring and funny and insightful and human, not just honest and professional and informative. That subtracts nothing from their ability to tell hard truths. In fact, it improves the ability to tell hard truths—and have them accepted and believed."[3]

The way in which Batten reconceptualized the role of newspapers—warm, caring, funny, insightful, human—expressed a growing realization among editors and journalists that newspapers needed to open themselves to a wider spectrum of functions beyond the one of solely being a watchdog if they wanted to stay relevant. Moreover, Batten explicitly forged a connection between this evolving role of the newspaper and the industry's capability to sustain its credibility and legitimacy.[4] These topics would preoccupy the newspaper industry throughout the 1990s and they would create fertile ground for narrative journalism's evolution in daily news production. But this kind of people-centered approach to writing and reporting would also need to find its place in a changing marketplace for newspapers. Business pressures would increase throughout the 1990s, creating opportunities for branding narrative journalism as premium content on the one hand, but also elevating the risk that narrative writing could be reduced to the lowest common denominator of banal entertainment. How did narrative reporters and editors situate themselves in this environment and how were they discursively constructing the purpose and the boundaries of narrative journalism in newspaper practice?

This chapter begins with an overview of the business environment of newspapers in the late 1980s and how it affected the content and makeup of daily papers. Propelled by a desire to "make the news popular"[5] again, reporters and editors were negotiating the parameters of when, where, and how to narrativize their stories—importantly, in ways we have not appreciated—not just in feature sections but in news sections as well. In particular, I argue against the common view that narrative journalism was little more than a gimmick devised to advance the "upscaling" of newspapers by reaching a more affluent clientele.[6] In my previous two chapters, I described how journalists introduced narrative techniques and discursively constructed their legitimacy in daily news production. In this chapter, I turn to analyzing how and why these narrative news logics began playing a dominating role in U.S. newspapers. To examine these changes in more granular detail, I then turn to a close-up look at one newspaper, the *Oregonian*, which gradually became a textbook case for adopting narrative journalism into daily newspaper routines. By focusing on the transformation of one newsroom over the course of about ten years, this analysis illustrates how organizational change and institutional change were interlinked in the development of narrative journalism. The next section shows how, at the same time, professional conventions, conferences, and workshops helped construct a common identity among practitioners of narrative journalism. This community of practice fostered relationships between proponents of the form, galvanized the imagination of young reporters, canonized theory and practice, and established narrative writing as an institutional fixture in American journalism. At the end of the chapter, I discuss the relationship—and the persisting tensions—between these forms of narrative journalism and the business imperatives they purported to address.

The Changing Marketplace

At the same time that editors were rethinking the editorial side of newspapers in the early 1990s, executives on the business side were intensifying their efforts to improve marketing, circulation, and appeal for advertising. After the 1980s—a decade of technological change, accelerating mergers and acquisitions, and the rise of new competitors (cable television) with even newer ones on the horizon (internet)—the newspaper industry was still grappling to find a compelling strategy to fight back against the structural circulation loss. There were fewer newspapers in 1989 than in the early 1970s (1,626 in 1989 compared to 1,748 in 1970). Total circulation for morning and evening newspapers had stagnated (62,649,218 vs. 62,107,527), while it had increased for Sunday newspapers (62,008,154 vs. 49,216,602). But even this significant increase could not make up for the relative loss of the daily newspaper audience. The percentage of newspaper readers had dropped from 78 percent to 64 percent during the week and from 72 percent to 67 percent on Sundays.[7] Profits were still handsome, but among business leaders and editors anxiety was growing that the long-term survival of newspapers might be in jeopardy.[8] Moreover, the newspaper industry was part of larger forces in the U.S. economy during the 1980s pushing businesses toward market specialization involving "systematic attempts by manufacturers to create slightly different versions of the same products in order to aim at different parts of the marketplace."[9]

These external and internal business forces had already created pressures on newspaper editors and led many of them to make substantial changes in content and presentation. Addressing the American Society of Newspaper Editors in 1988, Leo Bogart, one of the industry's foremost researchers during that period, summed up the significant changes between 1983 and 1988, many of which had ramifications for the evolution of a more segmented audience. According to Bogart, the news hole in newspapers had grown significantly, leading to "more pages for editors to fill and more pages for readers to contend with." The trend "to package editorial matter in terms of clearly definable and identifiable sections" had continued. And overall, there was "more emphasis on features and entertainment relative to news information, and more emphasis on local as opposed to national and world news."[10] These changes had not only transformed the look and content of newspapers but also the relationship with their audiences. As the one-size-fits-all approach to reach a mass audience began to lose appeal, newspapers began assembling their audiences by targeting specific demographic groups.

Following the logic of market segmentation, as Thomas Leonard pointed out, newspapers largely gave up on reaching a mass audience and instead focused on more privileged subscribers and elite readers.[11] As a consequence, many newspapers were no longer prioritizing the winning over of nonreaders but cultivating existing or potential readers that were most desirable to advertisers.[12] "We'll go after people who are interested in us," explained *Minneapolis Star Tribune* publisher Joel Kramer, "with a high-quality presentation of the news. We won't invest a lot of money on games and gimmicks for people who basically don't want the paper. We'll spend more to make it worth the money for our readers/subscribers."[13] Kramer's view resonated with ASNE-sponsored research that identified a prime target audience of "potential readers" who were described as "young, bright, busy and eager to learn more." Other categories in this 1990 study (conducted by Minnesota Opinion Research, Inc.) included "loyal readers," "poor prospects," and "at-risk readers." The group of loyal readers made up more than half of readers, but their numbers were shrinking and most of them were older in age. "Poor prospects," in other words, infrequent readers unlikely to become subscribers, and "at-risk readers," people who preferred broadcast news but read regularly, amounted to about one-third of the population.[14] Although potential readers constituted a mere sixth of the overall population, they were the ones that newspapers began targeting. The rationale for zeroing in on them and ignoring the rest was guided by the belief that advertisers could tolerate a relative loss in overall readership if, simultaneously, the remaining portion was younger, more affluent, and more educated.

Some of the biggest content changes in the late 1980s and early 1990s were driven by business pressures and the growing corporatization of newsrooms. Following larger trends in the American economy, mergers and acquisitions also dominated the newspaper industry. Family-led papers were sold to chains, and newspaper groups were bought by media conglomerates. As a result, editors were forced to think more like managers, and MBAs began ruling the newsrooms.[15] However, as Doug Underwood argued, these developments often led to diverging effects. On the one hand, marketing and strategic planning increased the pressure on editors to pander to the lowest common denominator and the needs of advertisers, leading to shallow and superficial fluff pieces. On the other hand, business constraints increased the consciousness of editors to focus on substantial improvements in quality, which meant "devoting more resources than ever to investigative teams and big, expensive projects designed to win prestigious prizes."[16] Moreover, emphasizing strategic goals and benchmarks on the business side of news production led to the tracking of successes and failures. Newsroom managers had more data at their disposal to determine what kind of content worked and what did not. In light of this business environment, many have seen the introduction of narrative journalism as little more than a tool to advance the upscaling of newspapers, playing into the hands of business executives whose goal was not to reach the biggest possible audience but the most desirable segment with the most value for advertising. According to this view, narrative journalism simply catered to an affluent and highly educated niche audience at the expense of appealing to a wider and more diverse range of potential readers. Others have suggested that narrative writing led to softer journalism and encouraged the production of gimmicky fluff pieces.[17]

My own view is that these familiar arguments are both too one-dimensional and too removed from the "on the ground" conditions that newspapers faced, and the rationales they devised to legitimate their innovations. I would suggest thinking about the market, in the words of Christopher Wilson, not "as an external force which impresses writers with a uniform stamp" but as something that "exerts pressures within popular literary practice."[18] These pressures were not homogenous and led to different, at times countervailing strategies: journalists worked hard to draw the boundaries between serious and light entertainment, hard news and entertainment, and to sustain both general and more affluent readers. For some newsrooms, reaching the largest possible audience meant scale; for others it meant reaching a particular segment of the population. Moreover, while newsroom managers set the boundaries for creating content, reporters and editors had their own agendas in using new and more narrative techniques, and were inspired by a variety of motivations beyond the matter of profit. While some newspapers associated narrative techniques with feature and lifestyle sections, for example, others systematically implemented them in news sections. This schism, I argue, ultimately constituted one of the reasons that critics accused narrative journalism of being "soft." However, that charge conflated a variety of approaches into a single category. The actual pattern was more complex.

A Culture of Elevated Writing

Two decades after the *Washington Post* Style section pioneered the practice of narrative writing in daily newspaper production, many American newspapers had come a long way from shedding their gray and dreary writing routines. The collective strategy to improve writing in newspapers had already produced tangible effects. As a result of writing improvement efforts, the writing culture of newsrooms was no longer an exotic topic of conversation but a regular feature in industry interactions. The *ASNE Bulletin* still reported about initiatives across the country, yet the tone had shifted. Instead of merely legitimizing the need for improving writing in newsrooms, the magazine now routinely featured updates of ongoing efforts and descriptions of best practices. The magazine routinely carried articles about the craft of writing by senior editors, for example, a column named "The Write Stuff," that was first published in September 1989. Throughout the 1990s, other regular contributors were writing coaches like Don Fry and Kevin McGrath. The situation was similar at *Editor & Publisher*. That magazine also carried articles by writing coaches and provided information about studies that examined the impact of writing styles in newspapers.[19] In addition, writing committees both at the American Society of Newspaper Editors and at the Associated Press Managing Editors Association served as platforms to exchange ideas and facilitate conversations about what good writing was supposed to look like.

As narrative writing made inroads in daily newspaper production, it also diversified and found a home in different places. Paradoxically, since "narrative writing" was not a label that editors and reporters themselves used in their conversations, narrative *techniques* could be found in many places: in feature sections, for example, as well as in regular news sections. Over time, most feature sections emphasized service stories, "news you can use," and moved away from narrative techniques. Simultaneously, news sections supplemented their traditional news reporting with documentary news writing. This shift signifies the evolution from narrative writing as a niche phenomenon toward an established mode in daily news production even if the actual placement of these stories in the newspaper varied.

After the *Washington Post* had launched its Style section in 1969, lifestyle sections became an integral part of many American newspapers in the 1970s. During the 1980s, these sections took center stage and their expansion was mainly driven by business imperatives. "No longer relegated to the back benches of the newsroom or the distant recesses of the editor's mind," one editor noted in 1987, "feature sections today represent a pivotal tool in the growth of newspapers in their markets."[20] In an era of fierce competition with television and magazines, feature sections were seen as the newspaper industry's response to demographic, economic, and social changes. While the Style section pioneered the use of news features in lifestyle sections and emphasized storytelling as well as arts and culture criticism, feature sections in the 1980s were largely designed to focus on service journalism and entertainment. One features editor described the dual purpose of feature sections as providing information and entertaining the reader.

> By providing information that enhances the quality of our increasingly sophisticated readers' lives, critical assessments that help readers make intelligent choices on spending their money and time—consistently respected guides to the "quality keys"—restaurant, film, theater, music, art, television, fashion, food, wine, etc. And by entertaining the reader, holding his attention, making the reader know that the section provides a kind of enjoyment that can be obtained nowhere else.[21]

Editors, however, were not following one particular formula. Instead, they actively experimented in defining the role of feature sections in various ways. In fact, newspapers offered a wide variety of potential approaches and editorial strategies. The cover of the APME Features Committee report in 1988, for instance, illustrates these competing pressures poignantly. A cartoon depicts the "feature creature," a six-headed monster that is chasing after an editor. Each of these heads is yelling specific instructions at the fleeing editor: "Appeal to everyone!; Appeal to women!; Lighter! Brighter!; Heavier! Deeper!; More soft news!; More hard news!" This cover illustrates the spectrum of opinions, expectations, and business pressures. Depending on the actual example, feature sections could range from crude commercialism to sophisticated entertainment. They offered opportunities for substantial nonfiction writing but also propelled a certain predilection for fluff. This 1988 APME report provides a suggestive snapshot of what editors considered to be a successful feature story. The committee had asked its members to submit examples of "best features ideas that could be adapted and immediately put to work by editors everywhere." The final list of suggestions illustrates the tension between light distraction and deep storytelling.

To dive a bit deeper into these suggestions, I categorized them by relying on a simple definition of storytelling (a character encountering a complication that illustrates a larger theme) and examined their potential for a narrative approach. Out of the "101 Best Feature Ideas" only ten showed clear signs of storytelling—a clear indication that the word "feature" did not equal "narrative." Of those ideas that showed narrative potential, one employed the strategy of following one character over a specific period (e.g., a teacher's first week at school, an academic year in the life of a drama student, a year in middle school told through the eyes of a child) while others recommended a quasi-sociological or quasi-ethnographic look at particular groups or communities (e.g., an "in-depth look at the American family of 1988," "anatomy of a community theater group," or "Scout group or Little League Team"). One idea called for profiles of people in their work environment, "ordinary people who might not otherwise get into the paper." Two suggestions demonstrated a typical narrative approach of telling small stories that illuminated larger issues of crime and tragedy, respectively. In one of those, the *St. Petersburg Times* showed the example of a story that reconstructed how a man killed his wife and then himself one day after his seventieth birthday. "The key here," the editor wrote, "is to find such an event in which the participants had friends and family close enough to the situation to tell what happened and who are willing to be interviewed." The other example came from the *News and Observer* and the *Raleigh Times* and reconstructed the life of a homeless man who had frozen to death. "The reporter went beyond the surface to find out who this man really was and what led to his death," editor Marion Gregory wrote. "It showed the personal side of a man who otherwise was just a statistic."

The overwhelming majority of these feature ideas, however—91 out of 101—focused on themes such as travel, home design, fashion, real estate, the arts, and (local) celebrities. Many suggestions offered some kind of service journalism (e.g., finding support groups in the community, choosing the right diet, ranking of grocery stores). Several editors suggested story ideas for year-enders that recapped events in the community or larger trends in society ("Fads and fancies of the year"). Seeking active engagement from the readers was often encouraged through contests. One example by the *Times Herald Record* in Middletown, New York: "Pets are wonderful was the theme of a contest which drew more than 300 entries from children under 10, senior citizens in their 80s, and everyone in between."

Obviously this brief example cannot claim any generalizable significance. But it does illustrate the wide spectrum of ideas for what editors considered to be a successful feature section. There was no industry-wide standard for these sections other than offering some kind of mix between information and entertainment. Occasionally, narrative storytelling sneaked into the mix but overall, the feature sections focused largely on lifestyle issues. Paradoxically, feature sections carried fewer and fewer feature stories in the sense of narrative journalism and instead focused more on service-oriented articles.

By the mid-1990s, one features editor concluded, "A lot of features sections are getting very fluffy and overdesigned. They have a lot of graphics and not always a lot of content. They look great but there's no depth."[22] What this meant was that feature sections, the incubators of storytelling in the wake of the Style section, no longer carried the bulk of narrative journalism.

At the same time as feature sections diversified, however, narrative journalism was expanding in news sections. Flush with advertising dollars and ample space to fill, newspapers increasingly printed multipart series that explored a particular topic in great detail, often using a narrative approach. The serial publication of articles was not new, of course; the history of newspapers is full of examples. But the fact that newspapers increasingly used narrative techniques for these big projects broke new ground. These series typically found great resonance with the audience and often led to prestigious prizes. For example, a sixteen-day narrative in the *Baltimore Sun* that was heavily promoted increased the circulation by 3 percent and led to an ASNE award for reporter Jan Winburn.[23] These series were not only popular but also expensive to produce. For example, a six-part series by the *Providence Journal* about a surgeon who specialized in reconstructive surgery for genitals of children took eight months and was estimated to cost about $100,000.[24]

Reporters who wrote these longer pieces often invoked a perceived need to offer an alternative to the daily reporting. "The object of the series," said Ann Hull, a reporter for the *St. Petersburg Times* who had portrayed a public housing project, "was to shatter some stereotypes, to explore a subject that has been mythologized in mainstream newspapers, and that is a public housing project, racial tensions between the police and the citizens who lived in the projects." The series, then, was putting forward an analytical and explanatory approach through the use of narrative techniques while also aiming at engaging readers. Hull added that "we wanted to entertain readers as well. We were not shy about admitting that up front. We wanted to give readers a good read with a story that had a beginning, a middle, and an end, and instructed them along the way."[25] Thus, narrative journalism allowed for the synthesis of instruction and entertainment.

Despite their high production costs, series were not limited to big papers. In 1990, Terrie Claflin of the *Mail Tribune* in Medford, Oregon, won the ASNE nondeadline award for a story about a baby who had suffered from drug exposure while in the womb. Her narrative story was the last in a series of conventional articles. Claflin explained her motivation for the narrative piece as an effort to personalize a public policy issue. "I wrote several other stories about the problem," she said, "and what the medical community is trying to do, and what the legal community is trying to do, and the overall aspects of the problem."[26] These rationales parallel the developments that I describe in the previous chapter. At the same time, they illustrate how narrative techniques had become an integral part of what reporters perceived to be the most important, but sometimes overlooked, stories in their communities.

Narrative journalism also became one particular strategy for short news writing, capturing a personality or a specific news event in just a few paragraphs. In 1991, ASNE for the first time offered a writing award in a new category for short news (under five hundred words).[27] After Julie Sullivan, a reporter for the *Spokesman-Review* and *Spokane (WA) Chronicle*, won the award, she said: "In some ways, it is basic journalism, in terms of writing a good short lead and then staying out of the story—not telling the readers, showing them. Let the description tell the story."[28] Even though Sullivan described her writing as basic journalism, it actually flipped the traditional approach on its head. Traditional journalism stresses a more "tell, don't show" strategy while narrative journalism accentuates a "show, don't tell" approach.

Though narrative journalism moved from a niche phenomenon to a standard practice across many newspapers throughout the industry, it nevertheless required specific favorable conditions in individual newsrooms. To examine some of these conditions in more granular detail, I will now turn to the *Oregonian* and analyze how it became representative for adopting narrative journalism into daily newspaper routines. Arguably, the *Oregonian*'s adoption of narrative techniques was more sophisticated than what most newspapers were doing and eventually would win more acclaim than most newspapers could expect. But the core dynamics—an editorial vision informed by institutional change that was embraced by the rank-and-file—played out in similar fashion in many other newsrooms across the country.

The Oregonian

The *Oregonian*'s evolution from a relatively ordinary paper to a leader in the field began in the late 1980s and reached its peak in the early 2000s. For many years, it had served as the newspaper of record in Portland, Oregon, and had been owned by the Newhouse family and their company Advance Publications since 1950. Critics, however, often looked down at the newspapers in the Newhouse media empire for being "cash cows" and "old gray hulks of mediocrity."[29] Nonetheless, in the early 1990s industry observers noted a marked change in how Donald Newhouse managed his newspaper chain. He took on the role of chairman of the Newspaper Association of America and was elected to the Associated Press board of directors, thus acquiring more public visibility. Breaking with tradition, he hired accomplished editors from outside the company. By the year 2000, "the Newhouse Way ha[d] cachet," wrote the *Columbia Journalism Review*. "These are editors with reputations for excellence, and, given the freedom and support, they can be expected to create great newspapers."[30]

Sandra Mims Rowe was one of those editors. Within one year after she had taken over as editor of the *Oregonian* in 1993, the reviews of her tenure were already glowing. An article in the *American Journalism Review* applauded how she had accomplished "the most sweeping changes an American daily ever made over such a short time."[31] In the following years she transformed the *Oregonian* from a sleepy regional newspaper to one of the best newspapers in the country. An important part of that success derived from adopting and sustaining narrative journalism, the contours of which were developed by Jack Hart, a senior editor who eventually became the paper's writing coach and one of three managing editors.

Rowe came from a newspaper family. Her father edited a small-town paper in Harrisonburg, Virginia. After attending East Carolina University, she found a job at a Norfolk radio station and then moved on to the *Ledger-Star*, the city's afternoon paper. Later the company merged with the *Virginian-Pilot*, where Rowe began mainly doing news features. "I can't remember a time as an editor of the *Pilot* or the *Oregonian* that this wasn't important to me," she recalled later.[32] In 1983 she became executive editor of the newspaper and two years later the *Virginian-Pilot* won a Pulitzer Prize for general-news reporting.[33] When Rowe became editor of the *Oregonian* in 1993, she was aware of the paper's mixed reputation. In her view, looking back at it from the perspective of more than twenty years later, the paper was "satisfactory" at best.[34] Jack Hart, in fact, shared the sentiment that the *Oregonian* could be a better newspaper and do more with its resources. The paper, in his view, "was big, lumbering and largely inconsequential. It was a sleepy institution with a lot of died-in-the-wool newsroom politics."[35]

As editor of the Sunday magazine during the 1980s, Hart had been doing some training for staffers of the *Oregonian*. Before joining the *Oregonian*, Hart earned a PhD in communication from the University of Wisconsin and taught at the University of Oregon's School of Journalism. After deciding that he needed more practical experience, he went on a sabbatical and tested out working as a reporter, first for general assignments, then for the arts and leisure section. When he was offered the chance to take over the

Sunday magazine—"a sleepy, dusty corner of the operation without a sense for magazines"[36]—he seized the opportunity and gave up his tenured position at the university. Under his leadership the magazine thrived, became a regional (not just statewide) canvas, and won prizes. In 1989 he became the *Oregonian*'s writing coach and started the monthly in-house newsletter *Second Takes*, which was meant as a training tool and platform for editorial discussions. The following analysis is in large part based on the writings in *Second Takes*. The eight-page newsletter was published monthly between 1989 and 2001.[37] While Jack Hart did most of the writing, there were also many other contributors from inside and outside the paper. In addition to being a training tool and debate platform, this newsletter can also be understood as a rhetorical device. Hart, in his role as editor in charge of staff improvement, used the newsletter to persuade reporters and editors of specific goals, strategies, and writing philosophies. As such, the newsletter gives insights into the newsroom culture and reflects the *Oregonian*'s evolution between 1989 and 2001.

In the first issue, echoing the conversations of editors in the 1980s, Hart outlined the need for improving the newspaper against the backdrop of relative decline in newspaper circulation and the competition with other media for the time of readers. He also stated key principles that should guide the paper's effort in improving writing. "The first principle of communicating with words, pictures or graphics is simple clarity," he wrote, building on traditional values of newspaper leadership. Another principle, however, pointed in the direction of expanding core assumptions of what a newspaper should stand for. He wrote, "A newspaper's first duty is to inform but it also should stimulate readers, move them emotionally and call them to action."[38] This constituted a significant departure from the orthodoxy of most newspapers at the time, and positioned the *Oregonian* alongside other newspapers across the country that promoted a more interpretive, analytical, and also narrative approach to the news.

Introducing the idea of narrative writing in a traditional newsroom such as the *Oregonian*'s was a gradual process. The first explicit reference to narrative writing was in the fifth issue of *Second Takes*. Hart deplored that while there was a larger trend toward thinking about newspapers as daily magazines, only a few reporters had the skills to implement these techniques in newspaper features.

Not everyone's a raconteur, of course. And anybody who's ever attended amateur night in a comedy club knows that only a few rare talents can keep an audience laughing with a line of anecdotal patter. At some point skill with storytelling surpasses ordinary ability and enters an unfathomable realm we call art. Nonetheless, most of us can manage a successful around-the-water-cooler joke. And if we think about it, we also can isolate some simple rules of telling anecdotes that work.[39]

In one article, he wrote about the voice of the newspaper. After citing some examples from then-recent metro stories, he asserted that "most readers will conclude that our paper is stuffy, long-winded, formal, cold and distant."[40] In another article, he shared some thoughts from participants of a workshop at the Poynter Institute. One of those observations read, "Expand the definition of what's news: Become storytellers. Think about narrative form; think about second-person."[41] In this early phase, though, the main emphasis was on achieving clarity. After conducting a readability analysis of the paper, Hart made the point that "we all need to understand that while readable writing may be simple, it isn't necessarily simplistic." He also stressed that some of the paper's best writers were great storytellers because they placed value on clear, concise expression.[42]

One year after the writing improvement program had started, Hart summed up the training and coaching activities at the paper: The senior editors did daily critiques of the newspaper, and the writing coach had become a permanent position. Examples of good writing were featured in the newsletter, on a bulletin board, and in group discussions. Reporters had one-on-one sessions with the writing coach and completed weekly consultations, readings, and exercises. An internal library provided books and manuscripts on good writing. "The general impression is that our writing is clearer and clearer," Hart wrote. "The language is less dense, and *The Oregonian* sounds less forbidding."[43] One particular achievement that Hart highlighted was the use of leads that differed from the habitual reliance on the inverted pyramid style. "A quick scan of the local news columns suggests that we're being far more imaginative these days. When appropriate, we create leads by turning to anecdotes, scene-setters, wordplay, metaphor, vignettes, and even more original ways of getting into stories."[44] He mentioned that while previously one out of five local stories began with nontraditional ledes, currently that ratio was one out of three.[45]

Around that time Jim Camin, assistant managing editor for news at the *Oregonian*, reported the results from a feedback round at the American Press Institute. He wrote that several editors "thought the paper too somber throughout" and commented on not enough features, especially local ones. He mentioned that the critics praised one of the writing samples and "called it compelling, well-written, informative. But they characterized everyday staff stories as 'not exceptional.'" Overall, these editors described the *Oregonian* as "solid, organized, well-rounded" but also "lack[ing] a personality."[46]

To improve the quality of news writing, Hart also tapped into a growing network of writing coaches across the country. He brought in Paula LaRocque to critique the paper, teach a session on storytelling techniques, and have conversations with reporters and editors. As I explain in chapter 3, the role of the writing coach had significantly gained in importance ever since the early efforts of Roy Peter Clark at the *St. Petersburg Times* and Don Murray at the *Boston Globe* in the late 1970s. And the number of writing coaches had risen, too. After the first writers' coach workshop at the Poynter Institute in 1985, a group of participants wanted to continue the conversation through a quarterly newsletter. The first issue of the *Coaches' Corner* was published in the same year, and two years later the mailing list had grown from thirty-five coaches to more than eighty. Printing and distribution were paid by Poynter. The newsletter, too, served as a platform to build and sustain a network of dedicated writing experts in the world of newspapers.[47] Hart drew frequently from this community to fill the pages of *Second Takes*. The newsletter reprinted columns from writing coaches, reported about activities in other newsrooms, and provided hands-on examples for improving writing. Out of all these activities evolved a more pronounced strategy to discuss and promote narrative writing at the newspaper.

The next phase of the writing improvement program focused on educating reporters and editors about narrative writing more specifically. In an article titled "Missed Opportunities: Finding Stories behind the News," Hart acknowledged that by publishing a newspaper "our first public obligation is a full and fair accounting of the day's news." Yet, he asserted, there were other obligations, too. "A newspaper links readers and the rest of humanity, helping to make life meaningful by exploring the nuances of the human condition. When it does that, news writing serves the same purpose as literature. The great novels earned their status as classics because they used sophisticated story forms to reveal central truths about the human experience."[48] And Hart offered a simple template to illustrate his understanding of what constituted true storytelling in the newspaper: "a good story will—at the least—display these minimum characteristics: (1) an interesting central character who (2) faces a challenge or is caught up in a conflict and whose (3) situation changes as (4) action takes place in (5) an engaging setting." It is important to underscore that Hart was actively trying to change the traditional newspaper routines when he began introducing a systematic approach to identifying and writing narrative stories in the constraints of daily newspaper production. The way in which he made his argument shows that it was by no means obvious to editors and reporters that some stories differed from the inverted pyramid formula and thus required a different reporting and writing approach.

Hart's most systematic effort in laying out the idea and importance of storytelling in the daily newspaper appeared in August 1991. "[T]he story lies somewhere in the roots of our humanity," Hart wrote, and stated that storytelling was being rediscovered by newspapers. He detected a "nationwide movement to bring back the old way" of storytelling and made references to "writing gurus" such as Jon Franklin and William Blundell as well as to training efforts at the Poynter Institute, the American Press Institute, and newsrooms across the country. In fact, he was situating his own efforts in a larger ecosystem of narrative writing proponents. Hart was also keen to link the qualities of storytelling to a business rationale. "The idea behind all this is that tried-and-true story forms will help newspapers compete with other media. That kind of more effective competition, runs the argument, may help boost circulation."[49] Nevertheless, Hart was aware that introducing storytelling in a newsroom setting would face obstacles. "Literary-style storytelling isn't always well-received in a newsroom."[50] Hart also noted that storytelling was not part of newsroom lore, not taught in journalism schools, and not discussed in standard newswriting texts.

After the arrival of Sandy Rowe in 1993, narrative writing received the full editorial support of the newsroom leadership. Rowe brought a particular vision to the newspaper. She wanted to rekindle a "fundamental rethinking of what our obligation is to our reader, and how we can best fulfill it."[51] Her core convictions were that the paper needed more emotion and a more human touch. Hart blended these ideas with his promotion of narrative writing. And this emphasis on storytelling was further underscored after Rowe hired Jacqui Banaszynski, who had won a Pulitzer Prize in feature writing in 1984, as senior editor in 1994. In retrospect, Rowe underscored the importance of having Hart and Banaszynski define the narrative mission of the paper. "These were two people," she said, "who knew how to teach, who knew how to coach. Reporters who had those instincts [for narrative storytelling] were drawn to them. I consider what I did setting the stage and making it clear what kind of newspaper we wanted to be back in the '90s and creating the culture in which we could do that."[52]

One of Rowe's first directives was to get more profiles into the paper. As Hart saw it, "instead of boring readers with dry facts about government process, we should strive to show them how events and issues play out in the lives of real people. That approach makes news meaningful. It exploits the natural human interest in seeing how other human beings organize their lives and cope with life's challenges."[53] He encouraged reporters to approach a profile by identifying a "strong central idea that acts as an overall organizing principle" for understanding a particular person. Finding this focus or theme, he argued, was "a professional judgment that goes way beyond the traditional idea of objective reporting."[54]

In another issue of *Second Takes*, Hart explained how and why Rowe wanted to see more emotion in the paper. "She wants readers to *feel* the life of their community in their newspaper," he wrote. "She wants the paper to deliver the same laughter, anger, sorrow and excitement that packs folks in the movie theaters, rivets them to the tube and sells slick magazines by the millions." Hart acknowledged that "most of us have to work a lot harder at capturing the humanity that's missing in the typical news story."[55] In order to find and write more emotional stories, Hart encouraged reporters to look out for sympathetic characters involved in emotional situations and then gather as much sensory detail as possible to make the reader feel the emotion. Hart contrasted two ways of reporting. He called the first "the scientific method, the European way of mastering man and nature." As journalists, he wrote, we "have been taught to obscure the raw world and immediately abstract general principles. We work inductively, transforming the specific details into conclusions that can be widely applied. When we leave a scene, we remember the conclusions, not the details that led us to them." In contrast, an emotion-generating writer would feel the emotion him- or herself. When encountering an emotional story or witnessing a situation that was wrought with emotion, Hart urged reporters to acknowledge these instances that elicit a personal emotional reaction and then go to the newsroom and put these feelings into words. This example, Hart's differentiation between two types of reporting, illustrates that the question of how narrative techniques offered a different journalistic epistemology was not abstract but had specific implications for everyday practices. Moreover, this definition of a more emotional approach to reporting also highlights that emotionality was not encouraged for its own sake. Rather, Hart and others advocated for the emotional approach to signal to reporters, "You have to feel to make other people feel." As a result, this and other calls for emotional storytelling highlight narrative journalism's capacity to create empathy and how it offers opportunities for readers to feel immersed and thereby more engaged.[56]

One example of what the newspaper considered to be a perfect case of this kind of approach was a story by Erin Hoover that appeared on April 30, 1994. Hart wrote that this story "on a Northeast Portland shooting drew enthusiastic praise in the morning critique because it represented such an original and emotionally compelling approach to the kind of tragedy that can become numbingly routine."[57] The story began:

> Nathan stands alone near the yellow police tape, his hands shoved into the pockets of his black Raiders jacket, hood pulled over his short braids. The 17-year old stares at the body.
>
> It is a young man he knew. Not very well. But well enough.

Hoover then wrote that the victim was gunned down while riding his bike and noted that the police did not know why it happened. Then she described various bystanders at the scene, offering brief sketches of their backgrounds, how they knew the victim and how they felt about the systemic violence in their neighborhood. At the end, she circled back to Nathan as he "stands alone trying to understand."

> He talks with determination about his own life. He says he's stayed close to God, but many of the boys he grew up with have gone astray. He says he dropped out of school but now plans to go to Portland Community College for his general Educational Development certificate and then major in interior design.
>
> He wishes he could change his world.
>
> "I want us to wake up," he said, looking at Taylor's body. "How many more black people have to get killed?"

Excerpts of the story were reprinted in an issue of *Second Takes* accompanied by a personal essay by Hoover in which she described how she had approached the story. As Hart wrote in a preface to the essay, "Erin's story was particularly significant because it demonstrated how the techniques Sandy is encouraging can be learned and applied. Erin's inspiration came from a [writing coach] Chip Scanlan workshop that had taken place less than a week before."[58] The workshop was titled "Storytelling on Deadline" and echoed one of the strategic goals in the newsroom. Looking back, Rowe said that she always wanted more storytelling on a daily basis because it would make the "most impact with our readers." She acknowledged that "it's hard to do, it's hard to pull off even with the cast of talent that we had. I was never satisfied with the frequency with which we did it."[59]

The third phase of narrative journalism's expansion at the *Oregonian* was in 1996 when, for the first time, one of the paper's writers was included in the *Best Newspaper Writing* anthology.[60] Within the next few years, reporters would win Pulitzer awards and many other accolades in the industry, cementing the *Oregonian*'s reputation as a writer's paper. At the beginning of this third phase, Hart reviewed the paper's efforts for writing improvement and detected a positive impact on the business side:

> We at the *Oregonian* pay more attention to the ways we craft and present words than most newspapers. We attend workshops and seminars. We have, over the past decade, invited every major American newspaper writing guru to critique and to instruct us. We hold classes and conduct discussion groups. And our steadily improving skill with language no doubt in some part accounts for the fact that our circulation is growing and our newsroom is expanding.[61]

He connected the paper's activities to other initiatives in the industry, noting the importance of ASNE's annual writing contest, the crucial role of Poynter in advancing writing training, and the newly established National Writers Workshops (see below). In the subsequent newsletter, Hart emphasized that a culture of learning was essential for surviving in a competitive media world. "In these threatening times," he wrote, "newspaper journalism will have to adapt or surrender its place as society's dominant news medium. That means shedding the most outdated parts of our old culture and adopting a new culture better suited to our times."[62]

Against the backdrop of increasing competition with broadcasters and the onset of online media, narrative journalism was part of the strategy to offer a different take on daily events. In one article, Hart explained that a particular kind of narrative background story was an effective tool to differentiate the paper's coverage from spot news. The "tick-tock" story was defined as "the detailed, behind-the-scenes explanation of the circumstances that produced the breaking news." Hart argued that "[a]s long as we have a monopoly on depth in a hurry, we'll have an eager audience."[63]

Another important change was that narrative was not limited to specialists. Reporters on different teams experimented with narrative techniques when the occasion arose, and oftentimes they were surprised by the results.

Jeff Mapes, a political reporter, documented the first year in office of Senator Gordon Smith. Looking back on this experience, he wrote, "I didn't realize it at the time, but I was entering the world of narrative nonfiction."[64] He acknowledged certain challenges of using narrative techniques for political profiles. Some readers, he reported, thought that the series of articles was too soft on the senator and came off as propaganda. Nevertheless, he embraced the experience and "came away convinced that narrative nonfiction is something that people like me—i.e., beat reporters in the daily reporting trenches—can do more often."[65]

With these transformations, of course, came new challenges. The pitfalls of improperly using narrative techniques became an issue at the *Oregonian* when a number of scandals rocked the news industry in 1998. Stephen Glass, a staff writer for *The New Republic,* was caught fabricating parts or all of twenty-seven of forty-one articles. Patricia Smith, a columnist for the *Boston Globe* and a Pulitzer Prize finalist, had to resign from the paper after editors discovered that she had invented people and quotations in four of her metro columns.[66] These and other scandals (which were not necessarily related to narrative journalism) triggered an internal discussion about the ethics of narrative techniques in journalism. After more than sixty reporters and editors, including Sandy Rowe and her leadership, gathered for a meeting in June 1998, the newsroom acknowledged that narrative writing raised special ethical concerns. As a result, writers and editors with a special interest in narrative formulated observations and suggestions for dealing with the ethics of narrative. It is worth presenting their findings in detail here as they speak to the specific challenges of making narrative journalism work in the setting of a daily newspaper.

1. Choosing to tell a story in narrative form ups the ethical ante. [...] Because narrative involves huge numbers of subtle and sophisticated choices, it's easy to slip into dangerous ethical territory. And it's easy to hide ethical lapses.
2. The ethical differences among narrative nonfiction and more traditional news forms are differences in degree, rather than in kind.
3. Narrative should be a means to an end, not an end in itself.
4. Scenic reconstruction poses special dangers.
5. Telling details are key to narrative storytelling, but they invite stereotyping.

6. Narrative storytellers have an obligation to understand the world from the viewpoint of their subjects.
7. Internal monologue is a minefield.
8. Indirect characterization is more credible than direct characterization.
9. Ultimately, we should follow the same reporting standards, regardless of the form the story takes.[67]

At the *Oregonian* and elsewhere, the focus on emotional storytelling eventually led to some pushback and second-guessing. In 1998, one article in *Second Takes* quoted Barbara King, director of editorial training at the Associated Press: "What began as a good idea for humanizing stories has often become its own cliché. So, let's use the writing device, but let's keep using it more carefully and more deliberately by making the people we use more integral to our story."[68] As a result, Hart calibrated the call for putting people in stories and specified good reasons for doing so: "It's absolutely essential that we humanize our stories; Cultural diversity. We need it on every level and from every corner; To bring in different points of view; To bring color into our stories, particularly with quotes, and in speech patterns; Because our best stories show, instead of tell; To increase readability; As an opportunity to develop our writing skills."[69]

After years of improving its coverage in general and the writing in particular, the paper's efforts paid off when, in 1998, Rich Read won the newspaper's first Pulitzer Prize in forty-two years. His award-winning story analyzed the economic crisis in Asia by tracing the production of French fries from the Pacific Northwest to Southeast Asia. One year later, the *Oregonian* won the gold medal for an investigative story about systematic problems at the U.S. Immigration and Naturalization Service and reporter Tom Hallman took home the award in feature writing "for his poignant profile of a disfigured 14-year-old boy who elects to have life-threatening surgery in an effort to improve his appearance."[70] Hallman had been a finalist in the beat reporting category in 1995 and in the feature-writing category in 1999. The paper won accolades in the trade press, being described as one of the best newspapers in the country.[71] In 2008, *Editor & Publisher* selected Rowe and managing editor Peter Bhatia as Editors of the Year.[72]

The *Oregonian*'s success story, of course, was not only about narrative journalism. But developing and perfecting the narrative approach to daily storytelling in a major metropolitan newspaper was a crucial component in the *Oregonian*'s rise to fame. As indicated, the paper also benefited from an emerging national movement toward narrative writing.

The National Writing Scene

The breadth and depth of the movement suggested by the *Oregonian*'s transformation increased throughout the 1990s, culminating in the Nieman Conference on Narrative Writing at Harvard University in 2001. Earlier in the decade, the National Writers Workshop had started out in 1991 in Wilmington, Delaware, when John Walston, then managing editor of the *Wilmington News Journal*, organized a writing weekend for journalists. Bestselling author James Michener was the keynote speaker as 325 participants sat in the audience.[73] Two years later the Poynter Institute came on board and provided national direction for the locally organized writing weekends. That first year, more than 3,000 participants attended the events—all happening on the same weekend—in six locations. There were more than 180 speakers, and the average age of attendants was under 30.[74] The target audience was young journalists from small- and medium-sized newspapers. The idea behind the gatherings was to combine keynote speakers and panels with one-on-one coaching sessions conducted by volunteers from the sponsoring newspapers. In the course of five years, 15,000 journalists attended one of the NWW's regional sites and interacted with 1,200 featured speakers and workshop leaders.[75]

The mission of the workshops included to "create for journalists the best possible writing training at the lowest possible cost" and to "help participants feel part of a national community of writers."[76] In order to attract major newspapers as hosts, Poynter touted that organizing a workshop was a "relatively safe bet. The most successful site made about $20,000. The least successful lost about $6,000. The average site makes about $3,000."[77] A typical program had twenty-four to thirty-two speakers and workshop leaders. There were general sessions in a large auditorium, large breakouts featuring three parallel sessions, and small breakouts of six parallel sessions. In addition, participants could sign up for twenty-minute coaching sessions with senior writers from participating newspapers. Once a year, Poynter published *The Workbench*, a newsletter containing highlights of the workshops, previews, and, in the early years, articles about writing.

The writing workshops were but one element in the changing public perception and appreciation of narrative journalism in the 1990s. In an article titled "Tom Wolfe's Revenge" for the *American Journalism Review* in October

1994, Chris Harvey took stock of narrative journalism's status in U.S. newspapers.[78] "A few decades ago," he wrote, "feature writer Tom Wolfe was pil-
loried in print for having 'the social conscience of an ant' and a 'remarkable
unconcern' for the facts. Only a visionary could have predicted his impact on
journalism would be lasting." But today, Harvey continued, "elements of the
New Journalism that Wolfe so tirelessly promoted have become as common-
place as the pie chart in many newspapers, ranging from the *New York Times*
to the *Oregonian* to the weekly *Washington City Paper.*" Wolfe himself had
detected a sea change in daily newspaper writing as early as 1990. Invited to
speak at the annual ASNE convention, he told newspaper editors:

> [N]ewspapers are beginning, quite instinctively and without necessarily any
> particular plan, to report these things in a quite sociological or anthropological
> way. I notice on the front page of newspapers now, more and more, I see more
> and more pieces that are sociological or anthropological in nature. The changes
> in the way people live are now front page news. It is terrific, and since I am
> being didactic, I urge everybody to continue this.[79]

Ever since his famous introduction to *The New Journalism* Wolfe had underscored that his idea of the New Journalism meant a more sociological and
anthropological approach and not just stylistic fireworks. Nonetheless, what
must have appeared to Wolfe as a vindication of his own efforts to challenge
old journalistic routines also shows that the evolution of narrative storytelling in newspapers was more institutionally based and collectively shaped
than is typically acknowledged. Moreover, addressing issues in a more sociological and anthropological way does not necessarily require narrative
techniques. At the same time, however, the inside, institutional efforts by
Jack Hart and others in the storytelling movement clearly demonstrate how
editors and reporters fostered a new journalistic culture of blending sociological and anthropological issues with narrative techniques.

In 1998 the ASNE writing awards celebrated their twentieth anniversary. Writing in the *American Editor* (the successor of the *ASNE Bulletin*),
Sandy Rowe, then the president of ASNE, praised Eugene Patterson for
having established an institutional vehicle for recognizing excellent newspaper writing. Rowe also emphasized the importance of the *Best Newspaper
Writing* anthologies: "In truth," she wrote, "these volumes are gems created
to be mined and given away. They are loaded with inspiration from gifted
writers. Copies should be in the hands of all reporters who aspire to write

memorable and moving stories and on the minds of editors whose job it is to create the environment and teach the skills that allow reporters to do their best work."[80] At this stage, the anthology had become more than a simple archive of award-winning journalism. It was strategically positioned to teach the next generation of journalists. As Roy Peter Clark and Christopher Scanlan wrote in the preface to the anniversary collection, "Our goal in collecting these pieces from the last 20 years of award winners was to provide students of journalism, from first semester news writing and reporting students to experienced working journalists, with exemplary and practical examples of the craft."[81] Another indicator that narrative writing had achieved a critical mass was that the literary marketplace offered opportunities for practitioners and proponents of narrative writing to explain their craft and provide tools of instruction. Books about narrative writing and how-to manuals became an important cottage industry and provided significant resources.[82]

Academic institutions, too, responded to an emerging interest in discussing and studying the practice of narrative journalism. In the fall of 1992, the University of Oregon's School of Journalism and Communication inaugurated the first full-fledged master's program for narrative journalism, called a master's program in Literary Nonfiction, that was located in a journalism school. In 1998, the University of Missouri's School of Journalism organized a conference under the title "Can Storytelling Save Newspapers?"[83] Boston University held annual conferences on narrative journalism initiated and organized by Mark Kramer. While the Poynter Institute continued its efforts to promote and teach narrative writing both in St. Petersburg and through the National Writers Workshops, the American Press Institute (API) also acknowledged the benefits of storytelling. Warren Watson, the director of API, wrote that he was "a new convert to the raw power and influence of this newspaper writing form." He urged editors to consider narrative journalism as an important strategy to engage readers, tell complex stories, and boost morale in the newsroom. And he also added a business argument. "At a time," Warren wrote, "when newspapers are faced with more competition from print and electronic media, when readers say they have no time to read, editors and publishers can derive benefits from adopting narrative storytelling as a major form."[84]

The narrative conference at Boston University and then at Harvard hosted by the Nieman Foundation became the highlight of the narrative journalism scene. It lent legitimacy and prestige to narrative journalism as a craft and offered a platform to reflect on its theory, practice, and ethics. "We call it narrative writing," Pulitzer Prize winner Rick Bragg said at one point during one of the sessions, "because you would never get 800 people to come to a seminar on features. Let's face it. You'd never get Harvard to sponsor a seminar on feature writing. But you call it narrative journalism and you can get people from all over the world."[85]

The conference, most importantly, helped create a common identity both for participants as well as for journalists across the country, who learned about the debates through trade publications, journals (*Nieman Reports*), and word of mouth. While the National Writers Workshops were focused on training the next generation, the conferences in Boston served as the forum for leading experts and practitioners in the field.[86] In light of all these developments, Mark Kramer saw enough evidence to claim that "narrative writing is returning to newspapers." He cited the Associated Press's enterprise reporting team, efforts at "a few dozen papers" to "identify and free up reporters with a storytelling knack," as well as the National Writers Workshops and the conference at Boston where "self-identified newsroom renegades" gathered. Taken together, he concluded, "an unofficial 'narrative movement' has coalesced."[87]

The discussions at the Nieman conference among proponents and practitioners of narrative journalism reflected certain themes, illustrating how this community discursively constructed the practice of narrative journalism and imbued it with a civic purpose. Practitioners were, in fact, demarcating the boundaries between serious journalism and emotional manipulation while simultaneously elevating their own stature and authority. Narrative journalism, in their view, supported and expanded the civic mission of newspapers. As Kramer argued, "narrative [. . .] opens more material for reporting—the revealing, nuanced lives of not just the prominent, but of ordinary citizens."[88] Madeleine Blais echoed the sentiment that this approach had a clear democratic impetus. "Literary nonfiction," she said, "has a deep American backbone, fixed in the democratic notion that real stories about real people are worth telling."[89] Discussions also revolved around resistance to storytelling in newspapers. Some participants were cautioning against overusing narrative. "We mislead our readers," William Woo said, "when in the name of producing an interesting story we superimpose an arbitrary order on an incomplete selection of facts and present it as the reality—as the what that happened. In doing so I think we also can mislead ourselves into imagining—and even worse, believing—that life divides neatly into beginnings, middles and ends and plots and characters that develop as events unfold."[90] Some audience members were concerned about the impact of emotional stories as they might lead to the "creation of an anecdotally driv-en public policy."[91]

Overall, however, the conference allowed practitioners and proponents to define the terms of narrative storytelling and moderate the tension between traditional newspaper values and the possibilities of narrative techniques. No single document or contribution could encapsulate the variety and mul-tiplicity of approaches, but a particular eloquent example of making the case for narrative journalism came from Jacqui Banaszynski. It defined certain elements of storytelling and emphasized how narrative journalism served various purposes—communal, sensory, ethical, and spiritual.

> Stories are our prayers, so write and edit and tell them with due reverence, even when the stories themselves are irreverent. Stories are parables. Write and edit and tell yours with meaning so each tale stands in for a larger message, each moment is a lesson, each story a guidepost on our collective journey.
>
> Stories are history; write and edit and tell yours with accuracy, understand-ing and context and with unwavering devotion to the truth. Stories are music; write, edit and tell yours with pace and rhythm and flow, throw in the dips and twirls that make them exciting, but stay true to the core beat. Remember that readers hear stories with their inner ear.
>
> Stories are our conscience; write and edit and tell yours with a passion for the good they can do, the wrongs they can right, the truths they can teach, the unheard voice they can give sound to. And stories are memory; write and edit and tell yours with respect for the past they archive and for the future they enlighten.
>
> Finally, stories are our soul; so write and edit and tell yours with your whole selves. Tell them as if they are all that matters, for if that is what you do—tell our collective stories—it matters that you do it as if that is all there is.[92]

Conclusion

The Nieman conference at Harvard University constituted a moment in time when narrative news writing had fully arrived as legitimate practice in U.S. newspapers. The fact that the storytelling movement established such a distinct form of news in the course of three decades deserves particular attention, which the interpretive lens of cultural institutionalism helps to elucidate. For the most part, institutionalists have treated the form of news as a dependent variable, neglecting its productive dimension of bringing about and changing news practices. Cultural studies scholars, on the other hand, while thoroughly investigating the symbolic representations and cultural manifestations of the news, typically ignore how these cultural forms are embedded in social practices, organizational frameworks, and institutional constraints.[93] It is precisely this link between formats and practices that a cultural institutionalism helps to explore. The form of news, as Barnhurst and Nerone argue, "seems natural and pretends to be transparent"[94] when in fact it is always already structured and shaped by a particular historical environment. Thus, journalism as cultural form encapsulates both aesthetic conventions of representation and social practices of news gathering. Too often, these interlinked components of the news production process are treated separately. Moreover, form and style are crucial components for examining how readers and viewers use the news. Broersma argues, "Conventions concerning form and style are [. . .] essential to make people believe that a newspaper's representation of the social world is valid. They determine which stories are told and how they are told, and by doing so they determine how we experience the world."[95] Narrative journalism provided new conventions that conveyed information by emotionally engaging readers, offering a representation of the social world through explanation, analysis, and interpretation that was distinct from traditional news writing.

By the end of the 1990s, many journalists advocated for the same characteristics that James Batten had urged them to embrace at the beginning of the decade: to make their newspapers "warm and caring and funny and insightful and human." At the same time, however, as James Baughman noted, "there were unmistakable signs in the late twentieth century that many newspaper groups were diminishing their product. Most conglomerate-owned newspapers treated their holdings like cash cows. Pressures to maintain or increase profit margins intensified, often at the expense of content."[96]

Neither this chapter nor this book can give a definitive answer to the questions of how business pressures affected narrative journalism and whether these factors led to an upscaling of newspapers or a dumbing down of news content. My objective for this analysis was more limited. I explored how journalists discursively constructed the practice of narrative journalism in newspapers, highlighting their rhetorical strategies to justify what they were doing, how they were doing it, and why they were doing it. For the most part, narrative journalists were oblivious to business pressures and commercialization. The latter is defined by McManus as "any action intended to boost profit that interferes with a journalist's or news organization's best effort to maximize public understanding of those issues and events that shape the community they claim to serve."[97] From the perspective of narrative reporters and editors, the main goal of their endeavor was certainly not to boost profit. Nevertheless, they often made the argument that narrative journalism, by maximizing "public understanding of those issues and events that shape the community" *also* helped to boost circulation. Thus, they used business arguments to sell their approach to management and justify what they were doing. And numerous examples attest to the immediate positive economic effects (circulation) of deeply researched, well-written story projects.[98] At the same time, however, it is dubious that narrative journalism alone changed or would have been able to change the bottom line for newspapers.

Another area of criticism concerns the supposedly elitist character of narrative journalism and its role in advancing the upscaling of newspapers. As much as newspapers branded and promoted narrative journalism as premium content, however, they still wanted to reach a general audience and found that storytelling had a universal appeal. Reporters and editors were making the argument that in a diverse yet highly individualistic society such as the United States, storytelling in newspapers actually brought people together. They argued that narrative news stories offered a lens to illuminate universal themes in a fragmented social world, emphasizing the specific quality of storytelling to explore and elucidate the human condition. In a way, then, narrative journalists positioned their practices as a counterpoint to strategies of segmenting the audience. Their efforts were strengthened by readership studies that examined how and why readers preferred certain forms of content over others. These industry-sponsored studies had been conducted since the late 1970s and initially showed mixed results with regard to narrative stories. But when John Lavine, the director of the Readership Institute and the Media Management Center at Northwestern University, summarized a quarter century of research at the ASNE conference in 2001, he pointed out that on topics like "politics, government and war, [. . .] readers want greater quantity and feature-style stories." Findings also showed, he added, that feature-style writing improved the brand of newspapers, making them more relevant and more meaningful to their readers, particularly to women.[99] Moreover, when it came to local reporting, he said readers wanted "to know about all the stories you do through the lives of ordinary people. We should take ordinary people and do real stories about their lives."[100] These readership studies, then, validated claims of narrative journalists that readers in general wanted more in-depth, feature-style stories about real people.

American journalism, as Christopher Daly put it, is "a cultural enterprise lodged inside a business enterprise."[101] Therefore scholarship should be sensitive to acknowledge both elements and differentiate between cultural influences and business imperatives. It is also important not to fall back to a false dichotomy, prioritizing one or the other. American newspapers in the late twentieth century faced competition from other media and a wide array of additional entertainment options. But editorial autonomy exerted influence and launched specific content innovations. Narrative journalism was one of them—even if, at the end of the day, it was not powerful enough to attract younger audiences and halt the relative loss in readership.

My analysis here is not intended to refute the findings of political economists who studied commodification of news and the ideological consequences of a capitalistic market logic. Nevertheless, my findings suggest that despite increasing pressures to give in to business imperatives, newsrooms of various sizes and across the country found ways to exert relative autonomy. Moreover, as Robert Picard has noted, American newspapers in the late twentieth century were experiencing an "unusually lucrative"[102] environment. It is doubtful that narrative journalism actually made newspapers more profitable. But the profitability of newspapers certainly supported and sustained ambitious projects of narrative journalism.

CHAPTER FIVE

The Narrative Turn and Its Implications

W HEN AMERICAN NEWSPAPERS rediscovered storytelling between the 1960s and the 2000s, they broke with conventions, practices, and rules of traditional news writing and instead advanced narrative journalism as a tool of journalistic storytelling. This development coincided with but also reinforced a broader transformation of American journalism, a turn toward interpretive journalism. Across different kinds of media (broadcast, print) and across media organizations, journalists moved away from a straightforward chronicling of daily news and events and adopted approaches that emphasized analytical, interpretive, subjective, or contextual reporting. Narrative journalism added particular flavor and texture to these changes. In essence, it bridged the gap between explanatory and interpretive writing through storytelling: narrative technique that not only explains (makes something plain or comprehensible), but also interprets (presents or conceptualizes the meaning of events and experiences) by sometimes drawing from means of art and criticism. As reporters were turning their reporting into prose, matters of narrative form—the narrativizing and thus introduction of perspective and judgment—brought interpretation, subjectivity, and emotionality back to newspaper writing.

The findings of my study resonate with a number of quantitative studies that examined these different kinds of content changes.[1] Drawing on a sample of three newspapers, Fink and Schudson found that "conventional" news stories declined from 80 to 90 percent in the 1950s to about 50 percent in 2003.[2] During the same period, the proportion of "contextual reporting" on front pages grew from under 10 percent to about 40 percent. Fink and Schudson defined contextual reporting in a variety of ways: these stories may be explanatory, provide news analysis, or describe social trends. They may be based on numerical data or "engage the imaginations of readers, transporting them to unfamiliar places." Despite their stylistic differences, "all contextual stories share [. . .] an effort at offering analysis or context that goes beyond the 'who-what-when-where' of a recent event."[3] They also identified "social empathy stories," which they define as stories that "describe a person or group of people not often covered in news stories."[4] The number of such stories increased notably between 1967 and 1979.[5]

Comparing the coverage of immigration news in three American newspapers in the 1970s and 1980s with that of the 2000s, Benson found that the proportion of page-one articles with narrative ledes increased from 22 percent to 33 percent.[6] Weldon examined the front pages of twenty newspapers and found that between 2001 and 2004 the proportion of feature stories increased from 35 percent to 50 percent.[7] One of the most ambitious efforts to quantify the change in the content and form of news writing came from Barnhurst and Mutz. Analyzing the content of three newspapers over a period of one hundred years, Barnhurst and Mutz detect a fundamental shift toward more contextual and interpretive reporting. In particular, they argue that the "emphasis on interpretation and social issues increased substantially between 1954 and 1974" and that "reports became longer."[8] Another substantial study by Stepp, comparing the content of select newspapers from the 1960s to the 1990s, also documented how newspapers became more "featurized" during that period. "The bottom line is," writes Stepp, "that modern newspapers read different. They are, by almost any measure, far superior to their 1960s counterparts: better written, better looking, better organized, more responsible, less sensational, less sexist and racist, and more informative and public-spirited than they are often given credit for."[9]

As scholars explored changing styles, practices, and norms in American journalism, however, certain blind spots remained that led to three kinds of potential limitations: methodological, epistemological, and ideological. (1) Almost all studies that delineate a change in journalistic writing rely on content analysis. While this approach is indispensable for establishing a baseline for studying the changes in style, it is ill-equipped to take into account contextual factors of production, consumption, and presentation. Content analysis can tell us how one set of texts differs from another. But it is not capable of illuminating what practices, norms, and values led to these differences. (2) From an epistemological perspective, researchers have not sufficiently interrogated the knowledge claims of journalists. They more or less accepted dichotomous distinctions like hard news versus soft news, human interest versus civic journalism, information versus entertainment, without examining the conditions for these distinctions.[10] As a consequence, scholars arguably failed to notice the incremental shifts in journalistic styles and practices. (3) Ideological limitations are those that arise from normative expectations of what journalism should be. As Strömbäck and Salgado argue, interpretive journalism in and of itself is neither good nor bad. It depends on how it is done.

> If interpretive journalism focuses on journalistic interpretations and analyses of current events, including overt commentary, these interpretations and analyses can be well informed as well as uninformed, critical as well as uncritical, and providing context as well as distractions. This is, however, not a matter of interpretive journalism as a concept. It is an empirical not a conceptual matter. Normative assessments should hence be kept apart from the conceptualization of interpretive journalism.[11]

I would argue that the same is true for the study and conceptualization of narrative journalism. Suspicion and aversion of narrative techniques at times inhibited a more holistic analysis of narrative journalism and its particular characteristics in terms of journalistic practices, norms, and values. So what is the legacy of narrative journalism's evolution in the late twentieth century? And what can we learn from this study, an inductive analysis that traced how reporters and editors introduced and discursively constructed narrative techniques in news writing, about U.S. journalism more generally? After a brief summary of my findings, I discuss them in the three areas that I outlined in the introductory chapter and referenced throughout the book: journalism as a news logic, journalism as a regime, and journalism as a cultural institution.

The previous three chapters identified a variety of ideas and motivations that journalists invoked as they discursively constructed how and why the content of newspapers needed narrative elements. Chapter 2 showed how the *Washington Post* disrupted news writing conventions by creating a new section that would showcase narrative writing. An important element in this disruption was that entrepreneurial editors and journalists used the lower status of the women's section and feature writing to their advantage. Editors and reporters actively embraced the gendered form of feature writing and validated its use in news writing. Chapter 3 demonstrated how collective efforts effectively mainstreamed techniques that had been considered as being mostly part of magazines. Across organizations, reporters and editors discursively constructed narrative journalism as a legitimate form of news writing and mobilized material resources to create lasting structures. Making the story form work in daily news production required a deliberate effort to redefine the content and boundaries of traditional journalism, eventually fostering the notion of augmented objectivity. Chapter 4 emphasized how narrative journalists channeled economic pressures into opportunities, pushing their own agenda of establishing an interpretive community and creating a reform movement. Eventually, narrative journalism took shape as a distinct cultural form of news, adding a novel way of reporting and writing the news in daily newspapers. In addition to the traditional objective of journalism to answer the question of "What happened?," narrative techniques allowed reporters and editors to address the questions "What does it mean?" and "How does it feel?" Taken together, this institutional history illustrates the emergence of a new set of occupational norms (e.g., mindfulness, emotional involvement, empathy) that challenged and undermined traditional conceptions of objectivity and detachment.[12]

Cultural Institutionalism

As I have analyzed the changing culture of storytelling and news, it is now my goal to illustrate how this fundamental shift in news culture can be examined through the lens of cultural institutionalism, blending elements from institutional theory and cultural inquiry.

Institutionalism as a theoretical approach in the social sciences has experienced a renaissance in the last three decades. Shedding the historical baggage from earlier attempts of conceptualizing institutions, the new institutionalism planted particularly strong roots in political science and sociology.[13] There are different iterations and the foci of analysis vary across disciplines but at its most basic level, institutionalists share the assumption that institutions are key components of human life in that they sustain and structure social interactions.

> An institution is a relatively stable collection of rules and practices, embedded in structures of *resources* that make action possible—organizational, financial and staff capabilities, and structures of *meaning* that explain and justify behavior—roles, identities and belongings, common purposes, and causal and normative beliefs.[14]

Within journalism and media studies, conceptual frameworks of institutionalism typically theorize media as a political institution. Most scholars are interested in examining how and to what extent journalism is connected to and constrained by other institutions in society (i.e., government, law, the marketplace, etc.). They are especially keen to observe how these dynamics affect the quality of public deliberation and the role of journalism in democratic societies. Institutionalists like Cook, Sparrow, Kaplan, and Ryfe have made important contributions to media and journalism studies in recent years.[15] Their scholarship builds on the notion that news making is a collective process yielding a relatively homogenous product of packaged information. As Cook wrote, "The literature is remarkably consistent in its portrayal of what news is and how it gets produced. Differences are ones of degree rather than kind."[16] This kind of analysis rejects both voluntaristic models that prioritize agency as well as organizational models that explain journalistic practice by the structural settings of news organizations. Institutionalists argue that what really defines journalism and its routines are institutions, not individual initiatives or organizational practices. In their view, the homogenous character of news production—in terms of sources, representation, formats—demonstrates how options for individual initiatives are highly limited and constrained; at the same time, they argue that the homogeneity of the news cannot be explained by organizational practices alone. Journalists, in this view, are not so much autonomous agents as institutional mediators that enact institutional norms, values, and role models. While institutionalists differ on whether journalism is more influenced by economic forces (Sparrow) or political forces (Cook, Kaplan, Ryfe), Ryfe identified a number of key elements that theorists agree on:[17] (1) Institutions mediate how macro-level forces constrain and shape micro-level action. (2) The institutional order is characterized by path dependency and a tendency to perpetuate existing patterns of social organization. (3) Timing and sequence of events and processes are crucial in determining outcomes of social action. (4) Institutions go through different phases during their life history. (5) Institutions emerge and dissolve according to the principle of punctuated equilibrium. Absent outside shocks, institutions display a remarkable stability. Yet, at critical junctures and during times of uncertainty, opportunities for changes and new directions arise that eventually lead to a reconfiguration of the institutional regime. However, despite institutionalism's theoretical insights, some scholars also expressed concerns that the homogeneity hypothesis might have been taken too far. As the late Tim Cook reflected,

"Certainly, powerful conditions push toward homogeneity across news outlets, and one news outlet is sometimes uncannily similar to the next. But we
should not take an institutional focus to suggest identical or complementary
coverage across all news media."[18]

Cultural inquiry has taken a wide variety of different forms over the past
decades but in journalism and media studies it is impossible to deny the
influence of James Carey. Carey turned to cultural studies because of his
frustration with behaviorist modes of studying the media.[19] While the
media-effects tradition may have been his nemesis—he called it "a failure
on its own terms, [. . .] antidemocratic and at odds with the professed beliefs
of its practitioners"[20]—Carey didn't spare other theoretical approaches from
criticism. He found political economy and Marxism insufficient as they re-
duce the richness of symbolic forms to the examination of economic structures.[21] As they claim that social structures lead to particular ideologies, they
take a shortcut from the source to the effect without acknowledging a sphere
where meaning is created, maintained, and transformed.[22] Carey assailed
functionalism for a similar form of reductionism. "Functional analysis, like
causal analysis, goes directly from the source to the effect without ever seriously examining mass communication as a system of interacting symbols
and interlocked meanings that somehow must be linked to the motivations
and emotions for which they produce a symbolic outlet."[23] Looking back
at his early critiques of functionalist sociology and behaviorist psychology,
Carey later explained that he had wanted to shake up the rigid boundaries
of media studies as an academic discipline: "[I]t was necessary to write such
things at that time to try to clear some space in the academy so other things
could be done."[24] Contemporary efforts to study journalism through the lens
of cultural inquiry focus on analyzing journalists as producers of culture.
By reporting, writing, and circulating articles, journalists do overt symbolic
cultural work.[25] "Analysis here," observes Zelizer, "considers the meanings,
symbols and symbolic systems, rituals, and conventions by which journalists
maintain their cultural authority as spokespeople for events in the public
domain."[26]

Let me now clarify how conceptualizations of cultural inquiry add important dimensions to institutionalism. While I embrace the general thrust
of institutionalist insights, my theoretical approach differs in two important aspects: First, as much as I agree that economic and political factors are
indispensable for understanding media routines, they do not do justice to

journalism as *cultural* practice. Schudson distinguishes two crucial elements of a "cultural model of media influence": first, media help "to construct a community of sentiment" and second, culture affects the media's capacity "to construct a public conversation."[27] In this latter context "[c]ulture is the language in which action is constituted, rather than the cause that generates action."[28] Focusing on journalism as cultural practice also means taking into account the perspective of its practitioners. At the same time, I am careful not to prioritize the experience of news workers. This approach is inspired by Zelizer, who highlights the inherent tension between self-perceptions and outside perspectives of journalists. "Cultural inquiry," she argues, "forces an examination of the tension between how journalism likes to see itself and how it looks in the eyes of others, while adopting a view of journalistic conventions, routines, and practices as dynamic and contingent on situational and historical circumstance."[29]

Second, in contrast to the new institutionalists who are mainly interested in interactions between the macro- and the meso-level (even though they also pay attention to individual attitudes and roles), I put more emphasis on the interplay between factors on the meso- and micro-levels. My approach is informed by the work of Wilson, who studied the rise of realism in literature and journalism in the late nineteenth century. His goal was to describe the emergence of a new literary form in journalism in literary, occupational, and cultural terms. At the core of his approach lies the notion that journalists are "cultural mediators" whose "social practice is intimately tied to historical needs, options, and opportunities."[30]

> By focusing down on individual writers my larger intention is to provide a more textured and flexible portrait of how mass culture is generated. We cannot fully appreciate the complexity of cultural institutions unless we populate them with human beings, or until we recognize the way in which, even as this market helped to formulate a "mainstream" or dominant style, it did so partly by selecting and amplifying certain *prior* cultural needs and aspirations among writers and audiences.[31]

I understand cultural institutionalism as a model in the sense that it serves as "an intellectual construct which simplifies reality in order to emphasize the recurrent, the general and the typical, which it presents in the form of clusters of traits and attributes."[32] As institutional and cultural dynamics intersect in myriad ways, I differentiate between three clusters in which news workers articulate and mediate institutional and cultural values. Those clusters reflect different dimensions of what cultural institutionalism in the field of journalism may look like: journalism as news logic, journalism as media regime, and journalism as cultural institution.

The Impact of Narrative Journalism
Narrative Journalism as News Logic

Narrative journalism has a long history, but in the last quarter of the twentieth century U.S. journalists actively constructed conventions of form and style to meet the needs and requirements of newspaper journalism. Reporters and editors "rediscovered" narrative techniques for a variety of reasons. Often, driving forces were their individual interests in reading and writing as well as some desire to combine journalistic work with literary flair. Many of these newspaper journalists found inspiration in the New Journalists, who themselves had found inspiration in the short stories of fiction writers or the older traditions of realism and naturalism from the nineteenth century. They were drawing from a rich literary tradition based on what Thomas Connery called the "paradigm of actuality."[33]

Yet, despite these literary precursors and the appeal of the New Journalism, the newspaper world presented significant challenges for practicing narrative journalism. This environment was very different from the freewheeling magazine world or the more eclectic publishing industry. The newspaper was an industrially manufactured product that had to be created and delivered daily. Its routines were based on the relatively inflexible technology of the printing press and on an occupational ideology that prioritized objectivity and detachment. The language was expedient if not always efficient and for the most part not literary. If journalism was an "industrial art" (James Carey), then journalists had to satisfy both the "industrial" and the "art" part.

Reporters and editors looked for different ways of telling newspaper stories and found examples in magazines, books, and the alternative press. They adopted reporting strategies and writing techniques that were familiar in other areas of the literary world but then used them in daily newspaper production. While the form of narrative nonfiction was circulating in a variety of literary fields, journalists needed to actualize its potential for daily news production, in other words, reconcile the requirements of narrative technique with the necessity of producing a daily newspaper under the norms, values, and practices that come with it. There was no preexisting consensus about what this narrative news logic could and should look like. There was no established terminology to describe this emerging form of news. Some called their stories features, others referred to a variety of names such as trend stories, takeouts, and mood pieces, when they were in fact practicing narrative journalism. Some described their craft as writing nonfiction short stories, others wanted to create a newspaper that was more like a daily magazine. Narrative journalism in newspapers developed in a fluid way and emerged gradually from experimentation with storytelling formats. As a result, narrative journalism attracted individual writers by offering the possibility to do artistic work and use creativity, imagination, and craftsmanship.

To make this text genre viable, journalists had to adapt, expand, or break with traditional reporting techniques. Narrative journalism required a significant amount of legwork and the use of reporting skills that went beyond retrieving information through quick interviews. As the previous chapters have demonstrated, reporters often immersed themselves in subcultures and spent significant amounts of time with the subjects of their stories. In addition to establishing the facts, reporters strove to explore the meaning of events and experiences they were covering. To build trust and relationships with their sources, they had to show empathy and trust their own emotional response, a very different approach from the detached reporter who was supposed to stay above the fray. In turn, these new reporting techniques expanded the stylistic variety of journalistic writing while staying within the boundaries of nonfiction writing and respecting the ethics of daily journalism. In order to write like novelists, journalists had to think like fiction writers, yet at the same time also back up their observations with evidence from their reporting.

The narrative approach to news writing, as described throughout this book, affected all aspects of journalists' work: story selection, reporting, interviewing, and writing. As such, it constituted a different kind of journalistic epistemology and ultimately led to an emerging framework of norms, values, and beliefs. Initially, the narrative news logic was developing in various newsrooms for a variety of reasons. Over time, these practitioners learned of each other and fostered relationships and networks. As a result, they developed best practices, built a body of collective knowledge, and defined their own set of techniques. Ultimately, they not only expanded the range and content of daily journalism but also its objectives. The purpose was not just to inform the audience but to "stimulate readers, move them emotionally and call them to action."[34] Narrative journalism in newspapers became a journalistic genre that resonated with readers and gained prominence on award committees and across the industry. Journalists had become not just the chroniclers but also the "novelists of their time."[35]

This evolution of the narrative news logic illustrates that the form of news does not neatly map on a spectrum that runs from information (i.e., inverted pyramid) to story (i.e., narrative journalism).[36] Rather, it shows what narratologists have known all along, the intertwined character of story and information. "Stories," wrote Arthur Frank, "inform in the sense of providing information, but more significantly, stories give form—temporal and spatial orientation, coherence, meaning, intention, and especially boundaries—to lives that inherently lack forms."[37] Thus, when journalists adopted narrative techniques, they wrote stories in service of information, not in opposition to it. However, given the professional constraints and occupational values of journalism, journalists had to acknowledge the constructed character of storytelling, and thus potential tensions with regard to their self-image.[38]

Narrative Journalism as a Media Regime

As editors and reporters were constructing and legitimizing the form of narrative news writing, they were dealing with specific institutional dynamics within the news industry between the 1960s and the 1990s. The most important developments in journalism and also the most significant factors contributing to the evolution of narrative journalism were the rise of television and the commercialization of newspapers. As the previous chapters have shown, editors and reporters were not passive victims of these trends but actively mediated and channeled them according to their own ideas. Editors developed creative strategies (in accordance with or tolerated by) their publishers to modernize their papers, and narrative journalism became a significant part of this endeavor.

Narrative journalists, however, moved only gradually from their outsider status ("renegades," "weirdoes") toward being accepted and appreciated for their journalistic work. Fighting the stigma of producing "soft news," they created conditions for a different kind of journalism. Eventually, institutional support (ASNE, awards like the Pulitzer Prize, training institutions like Poynter) elevated individual initiatives to a critical level and helped disseminate models, templates, and exemplars for practicing narrative journalism in daily newspapers. After initial skepticism toward the influence of outside actors (e.g., toward college professors as writing coaches), journalists and editors for the most part embraced a culture of learning that was sustained by writing coaches, consultants, and training programs both within newsrooms and industry-wide.

The role of the American Society of Newspaper Editors cannot be over-stated because, by bridging organizational divides and rivalries, it provided resources, justification, and incentives for narrative journalism across the country. Events like the annual ASNE conference and initiatives such as writing contests played an important role in creating an institutional infrastructure for narrative journalists to learn from each other and develop shared norms, values, and practices. In addition, publications such as the *ASNE Bulletin, Editors' Exchange,* and *Coaches' Corner* validated the practice of narrative writing in daily newspapers and allowed the narrative news logic to gain traction in the industry. Industry-sponsored audience and reception studies also contributed to increasing the appeal of narrative journalism in newspapers. Even though storytelling did not turn out to be the silver bullet for saving newspapers that many were hoping for, it clearly resonated with readers and expanded the range of reasons why people read newspapers. Time and time again, readers responded enthusiastically to well-done narrative journalism and urged newspapers to do more. As recurring scandals and individual transgressions of journalists highlighted the pitfalls of a narrative approach, reporters and editors over time developed an institutional response to formalize rules and enforce them.[39] These normative frameworks never amounted to a formal code of ethics, but they nevertheless constituted a body of informal laws that would be enacted and enforced by editors, fact-checkers, and peer pressure.

In constructing institutional practices and rules, narrative journalists also advanced a different set of institutional values, particularly with regard to the role of emotions in journalism. Narrative journalism subverted the dichotomy between rational and emotional discourse, demonstrating that informative content potentially benefited from being people-centered. As George Getschow put it in his introduction to *The Best American Newspaper Narratives of 2012,* "The best nonfiction narratives have an emotional goal— to move people and effect change. That can only happen when the story connects with the deepest core of a reader's psychological and spiritual being. The connection must be strong and deeply felt, forming an emotional bond between the writer, the reader, and the subject. Making that connection may be the hardest part of the narrative craft."[40] That connection also raises important questions that go beyond the scope of this book. If emotions in the media are not individual and private but collective and public, as Carolyn Kitch has suggested, we need to pay particular attention to how tears and trauma are constructed in familiar news narratives. The danger, according to Kitch, lies in describing tragic events as "unanticipated exceptions rather than foreseeable consequences of chronic social and political problems."[41] Nevertheless, with its emphasis on scenes instead of events, people instead of sources, and sequencing instead of a straightforward delivery of news, narrative journalism redefined the purpose, the practice, and the possibilities of journalism in daily news production.

Narrative Journalism as a Cultural Institution

Between the 1960s and the 2000s, journalists actively reinterpreted what journalism could do as a cultural institution. They often referred to the changing lifestyles of their readers in order to justify and promote new forms of reporting and writing. In a way, lifestyle became a heuristic to talk about social, economic, political, and cultural shifts as journalists reacted to broad and fundamental changes in American society in the late twentieth century. Lifestyles changed significantly during these decades and narrative journalism offered tools to address and understand these transformations.

In the late 1960s and through the 1970s, editors and journalists saw narrative journalism as a technique to analyze, explain, and illuminate issues such as racial inequality, the women's movement, and youth culture. But an emphasis on lifestyles also included examining the growing suburbanization of the country, the private sides of public figures, and collective phenomena such as trends toward self-fulfillment, spirituality, and religion. Of course, social analysis and commentary had been important elements of journalism before, but now they took the form of narrative storytelling (not just essays and editorials) and found a place in daily newspapers (and not just books and magazines). This explanatory function of narrative journalism further developed in the 1980s as journalists were trying to go beyond the dichotomy of being either an obedient press or an adversary press. Narrative journalists positioned themselves as social commentators, providing narrative accounts of social and political issues and how they affected ordinary people.

In retrospect, cultural historians and sociologists have identified a confluence of factors underlying these cultural changes that journalists were dealing with in the last quarter of the twentieth century. The United States experienced growing economic prosperity from 1946 to 1973, suffered through a malaise in the 1970s, and then picked up with the economic expansion, occasionally sidetracked by recession years.[42] The postwar economic boom and the GI Bill laid the groundwork for expanding academic opportunities and access to education and training. Americans became better educated.[43] The shape and structure of American families changed. Women entered the workforce, yet without a reinterpretation of the role of motherhood.[44]

Following the civil rights era, a culture of diversity was born, as minori-
ty populations became increasingly empowered and self-aware. Americans
were increasingly targeted as consumers and consequently developed attitudes and behaviors that prioritized consumption and self-fulfillment.[45]
Americans became more critical of institutions. All of these changes meant
that journalists had to engage with their audiences in different ways. Narrative journalism was one of the strategies with which reporters and editors
contributed to this response.

Journalists often invoked democratic ideals to make the case that good
narrative writing served democracy because it highlighted the complexity
of politics and how it affected people, something that could not be captured
by solely focusing on government and institutional actors. They constructed
narrative journalism as an exemplary way to humanize the news and illuminate universal issues of everyday life. Critics of narrative journalism contend that it prioritizes human interest at the expense of structural analysis;
dramatizes instead of illuminates; offers light entertainment instead of public service; and leads to trivial stories driven by a desire to please commercial interests.[46] These critics contend that American journalism has become
softer, more commercial, and more adversarial, causing harmful effects for
political life and public debate. Against this backdrop, the findings of my
analysis shift the interpretive lens. In contrast to reifying the dichotomy and
hierarchy between hard news and human interest stories, the findings of
this historical study suggest that news content, borrowing a concept from
G. Stuart Adam, runs on a spectrum between two poles: civic and human
interest. Adam distinguishes these two kinds of stories in the following way:
"the civic, having to do with politics, the conduct of public business, and the
administration of society's major institutions and systems; and the human
interest, having to do with events in the lives of individuals and the community of souls."[47] While there are certainly more or less pure forms of each
kind of story, there is also a wide variety of stories combining the personal
with the political, human interest with civic debate, the particular and the
universal.[48] "[D]ifferent forms of journalism," Benson argued, "are produced
by and help produce different types of democracy, each with their unique
civic advantages and disadvantages."[49]

However one judges the impact of narrative journalism on democratic life
in the United States, news as storytelling brought more emphasis on people,
their lives, and the way in which journalists can actively transform particular
chronicles into universal stories. This transformation began in the 1970s and
continues to this day. Narrative journalism has not gone away. Stories have

not gone away. But as the newspaper infrastructure has collapsed, narrative journalism is evolving into new formats and narrative journalists are exploring new platforms in the digital world. That is yet another story.

Methodology

My research is based on the analysis of documents, industry discourse, and oral history interviews. The methodological approach can be characterized as immersion and strategic analysis.[1] The varying availability and heterogeneity of source materials led to an eclectic approach that synthesized various research strategies depending on the specific analytical goals at hand. As a result, finding primary documents required strategic thinking and detective work, mining secondary literature for sources, and asking interviewees for cues, leads, and ideas. In addition, since I wanted to capture dynamics that affected the newspaper industry as such, I looked for ways to capture the institutional discourse and decided to focus on the American Society of Newspaper Editors with its publications and conference proceedings.

Documents were evaluated according to the criteria of authenticity, reliability, representativeness, and validity.[2] When analyzing documents that were circulated within news organizations (i.e., memos, reports) or industry associations (i.e., white papers, proceedings), I paid particular attention to situating these documents in their social settings, examining "how documents [were] manufactured and how they function[ed] rather than simply what they contain[ed]."[3] My rationale for examining the discourse in trade journals is best reflected in this description by Harp, who chose a similar approach for one of her studies:

First, there is an authenticity in the information [in trade journals] that is not spoiled by a personal recollection blurred by time. Second, the method chosen is likely to offer more summaries of the discourse, as this is the nature of written (journalistic) material. Finally, publishers, editors, and reporters throughout the country read articles in trade journals and, arguably, this discourse has an affect [*sic*] on decisions made broadly within the industry.[4]

I approached the interpretation of my source material as an iterative process. After reading through primary documents and interview transcripts, I noticed patterns emerging that increasingly finessed my interpretive framework. In lieu of a standardized coding scheme, I conducted an "organizational cultural analysis" as conceptualized by Driskill and Brenton. They suggest a specific analytical frame to identify "how organization members create values, norms, and metaphors."[5] These themes were then analyzed with regard to referential adequacy, in other words, "checking preliminary findings and interpretations against archived raw data, previous literature, and existing research to explore alternative explanations for findings as they emerge."[6] Finally, the analysis yielded master rules, paradoxes, and root metaphors, illuminating the organizational culture around narrative storytelling in particular news outlets and their variation across organizations.

My interpretation was guided by the research question: How did narrative journalists and editors discursively construct an alternative to objective, hard-news reporting? Of course, as this is a qualitative cultural analysis, I did not expect nor try to identify a specific cause and effect model. Rather, it was my goal to provide a "thick description"[7] of the newspaper industry of that era and identify norms, values, and assumptions that had to be negotiated by reporters, editors, and managers. Based on the theoretical model of discursive institutionalism that I outlined above, I analyzed the role of journalists as cultural and institutional mediators. However, my interpretation is also sensitive to economic and social structures affecting the range of individual and collective decisions. As Sugrue writes, "The consequences of hundreds of individual acts or of collective activity, however, gradually strengthen, redefine, or weaken economic and social structures. The relationship between structure and agency is dialectical and history is the synthesis."[8] It is my hope that my analysis provides a description of such a synthesis in the field of narrative journalism in American newspapers.

Notes

Chapter 1

1. Gaye Tuchman, *Making News: A Study in the Construction of Reality.*

2. Thomas Bernard Connery, *A Sourcebook of American Literary Journalism: Representative Writers in an Emerging Genre*; Connery, *Journalism and Realism: Rendering American Life*; John C. Hartsock, *A History of American Literary Journalism: The Emergence of a Modern Narrative Form*; Norman Sims, *The Literary Journalists*; Sims, *True Stories: A Century of Literary Journalism.*

3. Mark Kramer, "Narrative Journalism Comes of Age," 5.

4. Daniel Hallin, *We Keep America on Top of the World: Television Journalism and the Public Sphere.*

5. For example, Davies writes, "In content, newspapers began a long, slow journey to update their methods of reporting. The most significant trend during the two decades (after 1945) was the movement toward interpretation of the news. Rooted in the 1930s, interpretation spread in the 1950s as a response to the sensational rise of Senator Joseph R. McCarthy." David R. Davies, *The Postwar Decline of American Newspapers, 1945–1965: The History of American Journalism*, 129.

6. Kevin G. Barnhurst, *Mister Pulitzer and the Spider: Modern News from Realism to the Digital*; Kevin G. Barnhurst and Diana Mutz, "American Journalism and the Decline in Event-Centered Reporting"; Kevin G. Barnhurst and John Nerone, *The Form of News: A History.*

7. "The reportage genre is perhaps the oldest and throughout the history of journalism most sustainable journalistic genre," argues Steensen. As the New Journalism emerged in the 1960s, "history would repeat itself when journalists like Tom Wolfe and Gay Talese once again challenged mainstream factual and objective news." Steen Steensen, "The Intimization of Journalism."

8. Christopher P. Wilson, *The Labor of Words: Literary Professionalism in the Progressive Era*, xii.

9. Michael Schudson, *The Rise of the Right to Know: Politics and the Culture of Transparency, 1945–1975*, 177. Schudson does not dismiss the influence of the New Journalism entirely. He is careful to acknowledge that with its "brash outlook and

its bold attack on the stodginess of 'objectivity' in news [the 'new journalism'] was inspiring to many young journalists then and in the decades since."

10. Christopher B. Daly, *Covering America: A Narrative History of a Nation's Journalism*, 341.

11. Robert Fulford, *The Triumph of Narrative: Storytelling in the Age of Mass Culture.*

12. Barbie Zelizer, "Introduction: Why Journalism's Changing Faces Matter," 1.

13. Rodney Benson, *Shaping Immigration News: A French-American Comparison*, 12.

14. Barnhurst, *Mister Pulitzer*, 42.

15. John J. Pauly, "The New Journalism and the Struggle for Interpretation," 590.

16. An exception is the International Association for Literary Journalism Studies (IALJS). Over the past ten years, its members have shed light on new developments in literary journalism. Robert Boynton also made an important contribution in highlighting a generation of "new, new journalists." See Robert S. Boynton, *The New, New Journalism: Conversations with America's Best Nonfiction Writers on Their Craft.*

17. Kathy Roberts Forde, *Literary Journalism on Trial: Masson v. New Yorker and the First Amendment*, 56.

18. James W. Carey, "The Problem of Journalism History," 90.

19. Carey, "Problem of Journalism History," 91.

20. *Oxford English Dictionary Online*, s.v. "narrative, n.," accessed May 14, 2013, https://en.oxforddictionaries.com/definition/narrative.

21. John J. Nerone, "Narrative News Story," in *The International Encyclopedia of Communication*, ed. Wolfgang Donsbach, accessed May 15, 2013, https://doi .org/10.1002/9781405186407.wbiecn002.

22. Keren Tenenboim-Weinblatt, "News as Narrative," 953.

23. Christopher P. Wilson, *Reading Narrative Journalism: An Introduction for Students*. Boston College, https://mediakron.bc.edu/readingnarrativejournalism. My emphasis and addition of "emotional." See also Karin Wahl-Jorgensen and Thomas R. Schmidt, "News and Storytelling."

24. Chris Peters, "Emotion Aside or Emotional Side? Crafting an 'Experience of Involvement' in the News," 298.

25. Karin Wahl-Jorgensen, "The Strategic Ritual of Emotionality: A Case Study of Pulitzer Prize–Winning Articles," 139.

26. Chris Baldick, *The Oxford Dictionary of Literary Terms*, s.v. "convention," 2008, accessed November 19, 2018, http://www.oxfordreference.com/view/10.1093 /acref/9780199208272.001.0001/acref-9780199208272-e-251?rskey=lwCnRj&result =251.

27. Barnhurst and Nerone, *Form of News*; Horst Pöttker, "News and Its Communicative Quality: The Inverted Pyramid—When and Why Did It Appear?"

28. Elizabeth Bird and Robert W. Dardenne, "Myth, Chronicle, and Story: Exploring the Narrative Qualities of News," 69.

29. The distinction between "report" and "story" was first introduced to me as a heuristic by Lauren Kessler. I formalized it conceptually.

30. Baldick, *The Oxford Dictionary of Literary Terms*, s.v. "exposition," 2008, accessed November 11, 2018, http://www.oxfordreference.com/view/10.1093/acref/9780199208272.001.0001/acref-9780199208272-e-434?rskey=YPShdd&result=434.

31. Schudson, "Four Approaches to the Sociology of News," 181.

32. Schudson, "Four Approaches," 181.

33. Schudson, "Four Approaches," 59.

34. Vivien Lowndes and Mark Roberts, *Why Institutions Matter: The New Institutionalism in Political Science*.

35. Thomas Hanitzsch and Tim P. Vos, "Journalism beyond Democracy: A New Look into Journalistic Roles in Political and Everyday Life," 151.

36. See Matt Carlson, "Introduction: The Many Boundaries of Journalism," 6.

37. Peter Burke, *History and Social Theory*, 27.

38. Daly, *Covering America*, 338.

39. For historical context, see Pöttker, "News and Its Communicative Quality."

40. Michele Weldon, *Everyman News: The Changing American Front Page*, 1.

41. Benson, *Shaping Immigration News*, 208.

Chapter 2

1. Cheryl A. Skuhr, "Letter to the Editors," *Washington Post*, January 11, 1969, A12.

2. Memorandum from Thomas Kendrick to Ben Bradlee, ca. August 1972, Benjamin C. Bradlee Papers, box 4, folder 2, Harry Ransom Center, University of Texas at Austin (hereafter cited as the Bradlee Papers).

3. Handwritten letter from Katharine Graham to Ben Bradlee, ca. 1974, Bradlee Papers, box 164, folder 3.

4. James Fallows, "Big Ben," *Esquire*, April 1976, 53.

5. David R. Davies, *The Postwar Decline of American Newspapers, 1945–1965: The History of American Journalism*, 113.

6. As quoted in Davies, *Postwar Decline*, 113.

7. David Halberstam, *The Powers That Be*, 525.

8. Chalmers M. Roberts, *The Washington Post: The First 100 Years*, 394.

9. *Washington Post* stockholder report, 1973, n.p.

10. James L. Baughman, *The Republic of Mass Culture: Journalism, Filmmaking, and Broadcasting in America since 1941*, 187–88.

11. John Anderson, interview with Halberstam, the David Halberstam Collection, box 192, folders 5, 7, Howard Gotlieb Archival Research Center, Boston University (hereafter cited as Halberstam Collection).

12. Howard Bray, *The Pillars of the Post: The Making of a News Empire in Washington*, 105.

13. Lauren Kessler, *The Dissident Press: Alternative Journalism in American History*.

14. Bray, *Pillars of the Post*, 105.

15. James T. Patterson, *Grand Expectations: The United States, 1945–1974*, 368; Bruce J. Schulman, *The Seventies: The Great Shift in American Culture, Society, and*

Politics, 161. For an excellent overview, see Robert O. Self, *All in the Family: The Realignment of American Democracy since the 1960s*.

16. "The 'For and About Women' section was a power in the newsroom. . . . [The] editor was very powerful in her domain. You just knew that about her [Marie Sauer]. The idea of changing the section must have been an extraordinary thing to do." Leonard Downie Jr., interview with the author, September 28, 2015.

17. Judith Martin, interview with the author, June 17, 2016. Meryle Secrest described her as "tough as nails" but said that Sauer helped her a lot. Meryle Secrest, interview with the author, September 18, 2015.

18. Quoted in Mei-Ling Yang, "Women's Pages or People's Pages: The Production of News for Women in the 'Washington Post' in the 1950s," 367.

19. Judith Martin, "Before You Look Too Far Down Your Nose at 'Women's Pages,' Judith Martin Has a Word for You," *Washington Post Magazine*, December 12, 2014. These observations were confirmed by Meryle Secrest in an interview with the author, September 18, 2015.

20. Interview with Tom Wilkinson and Ben Bradlee on the creation of "Style," July, 6, 1993, Bradlee Papers, box 176, folder 9.

21. As quoted in Jeff Himmelman, *Yours in Truth: A Personal Portrait of Ben Bradlee*, 124.

22. "We were concerned [. . .] with the overall readability problem: how do you best organize the newspapers so as to give the reader the maximum ease in finding and reading what he wants to read in the minimal time he has to do it." David Laventhol, "Washington Post Thinks Style Is Stylish," 13.

23. As quoted in Kay Mills, *A Place in the News: From the Women's Pages to the Front Page*, 118.

24. Robert Gottlieb and Irene Wolt, *Thinking Big: The Story of the Los Angeles Times, Its Publishers, and Their Influence on Southern California*, 326.

25. For background on Jurney, see Rodger Streitmatter, "Transforming the Women's Pages: Strategies That Worked"; Kimberly Wilmot Voss, *Redefining Women's News: A Case Study of Three Women's Page Editors and Their Framing of the Women's Movement*.

26. Timothy Noah, "What David Broder Could Learn from Sally Quinn (and Vice Versa)," *Washington Monthly*, December 1984, 13. See also Marilyn Greenwald, *A Woman of the Times: Journalism, Feminism, and the Career of Charlotte Curtis*.

27. David Laventhol, n.d., memorandum to Ben Bradlee, Eugene C. Patterson Papers, The Poynter Institute. Note: At the time of my archival research in the spring of 2015, the collection was not formally processed and did not have a finding aid. Since then, the papers have been transferred to Emory University. Documents from the Eugene C. Patterson collection are identified as ECP.

28. David Laventhol, memorandum to Ben Bradlee and Eugene Patterson, October 11, 1968, ECP.

29. Steve M. Barkin, "The Journalist as Storyteller: An Interdisciplinary Perspective," *American Journalism* 1, no. 2 (1984): 27–34.

30. Elizabeth Bird and Robert W. Dardenne, "Myth, Chronicle, and Story: Exploring the Narrative Qualities of News," 67–86.

31. Nadler notes that "[c]ultural resonance may be a necessary condition for achieving popularity, but it is not a sufficient condition." I agree with his assessment that changes in content are also "a matter of *mobilizing* publics and creating new forms of feedback between news outlets and their publics." Anthony M. Nadler, *Making the News Popular: Mobilizing U.S. News Audiences*, 15.

32. Leo Bogart, *Press and Public: Who Reads What, When, Where, and Why in American Newspapers*, 151–52.

33. David Abrahamson, *Magazine-Made America: The Cultural Transformation of the Postwar Periodical*.

34. Ben Bradlee, *A Good Life*, 298.

35. Helen MacGill Hughes, *News and the Human Interest Story*.

36. Nicholas von Hoffman, "Women's Pages: An Irreverent View," 53. *Columbia Journalism Review* (July/August 1971): 53.

37. See advertisement, "The Washington Post in 1969," *Washington Post*, January 5, 1969, H54.

38. Michael Kernan, "Life Styles: The Mandels of Maryland," *Washington Post*, January 8, 1969, B1.

39. This reading is inspired by Christopher P. Wilson, *Reading Narrative Journalism: An Introduction for Students*. Boston College, https://mediakron.bc.edu/readingnarrativejournalism.

40. "One hallmark of a cohesive family is the dog, preferably one of long tenure. For the Mandels it was Sandy, a collie who was with them 13 years until his death a year ago." Kernan, "Life Styles," B2.

41. "Mrs. Onassis Explores Scenic Charms of Greece," *Washington Post*, January 3, 1969, B1.

42. Tom Wolfe, "The New Journalism," 32–36.

43. See, for example, Judy Bachrach, "Barbara Mandel: Time to Move On," *Washington Post*, December 21, 1973, B1.

44. My argument builds on Barnhurst and Nerone, who argue that the form of news has an impact on the content of news. "Form structures and expresses that environment, a space that comfortably pretends to represent something larger: the world-at-large, its economics, politics, sociality, and emotion." Kevin G. Barnhurst and John Nerone, *The Form of News*, 6.

45. For a discussion of the narrative form, see Bird and Dardenne, "Myth, Chronicle, and Story."

46. In literary terms, one could describe this technique as "tableau," a "description of some group of people in more or less static postures." It is worth noting that in nineteenth-century drama, this device was used in melodrama and farce, interesting connotations in this context of a political profile. Chris Baldick, *The Oxford Dictionary of Literary Terms*, 4th ed., s.v. "tableau," 2015, http://www.oxfordreference.com/view/10.1093/acref/9780198715443.001.0001/acref-9780198715443-e-1124.

47. Jack Hart, *Storycraft: The Complete Guide to Writing Narrative Nonfiction*. The 5 W's are who, what, when, why, where. Typically, "how" is added as a sixth element.

48. Martin, "Before You Look," 30.

49. Richard Kluger and Phyllis Kluger, *The Paper: The Life and Death of the New York Herald Tribune*, 606.

50. Bradlee, *A Good Life*, 302.

51. Kluger and Kluger, *The Paper*, 666.

52. Cited in Kluger and Kluger, 671–72.

53. As quoted in Robert F. Keeler, *Newsday: A Candid History of the Respectable Tabloid*, 448.

54. Ben Bradlee and Katharine Graham had a vision to make the *Post* among the most important newspapers in the country. "The demise of the *Herald Tribune* helped greatly. Until then, the customary iteration of the best papers was the *Times* and the *Trib*. Now a vacancy existed at the top that the *Post* was preparing to fill," wrote Harry Rosenfeld in *From Kristallnacht to Watergate: Memoirs of a Newspaperman*, 106.

55. David Laventhol, memorandum to Ben Bradlee and Eugene Patterson, October 11, 1968, ECP.

56. Wolfe, "The New Journalism," 21.

57. John J. Pauly, "The New Journalism and the Struggle for Interpretation," 591.

58. Robert Darnton, "Writing News and Telling Stories," 180.

59. Christopher P. Wilson, *The Labor of Words: Literary Professionalism in the Progressive Era*, xii.

60. "Sustained impact came from the typewriter of Nicholas von Hoffman, among those Bradlee hired in the spring of 1966. Over the next decade his vivid prose, often intentionally provocative, produced more angry letters to the editor than the work of any other single reporter in the paper's history. In the late 1960s and early 1970s he became a favorite of the New Left and of some of the youth cults. At THE POST some adored him; others considered him a menace to journalism. His contribution, until he began to fade after the end of the Nixon era, was substantial: by the very power of his words, the details of his reporting, and the outrage of his expressed beliefs he forced uncounted POST readers to examine a life style that repelled them, especially when it became that of their middle-class offspring." Roberts, *Washington Post*, 381.

61. "He was really the first narrative journalist on our staff." Leonard Downie Jr., interview with the author.

62. Von Hoffman, "Mule Wagon Leads March," *Washington Post*, April 10, 1968.

63. As quoted in Carol Felsenthal, *Power, Privilege, and the Post: The Katharine Graham Story*, 262.

64. Garry Wills, *Lead Time: A Journalist's Education*.

65. Memorandum from David Laventhol to Ben Bradlee and Eugene Patterson, February 2, 1969, ECP.

66. As quoted in Roberts, *Washington Post*, 404.

67. Memorandum from Katharine Graham to Ben Bradlee, Bradlee Papers, box 47, folder 1.

68. Katharine Graham, memorandum to Ben Bradlee and Eugene Patterson, May 6, 1969, ECP.

69. Katharine Graham, *Personal History*, 414. She went on to explain: "I tended to apply a dentist drill too frequently instead of considering things coolly and not constantly complaining."

70. Bradlee, *A Good Life*, 300; Graham, *Personal History*, 414.

71. Martha Sherrill, "Ben Bradlee: His Sense of Style Brought a New Sensibility to Features," *Washington Post*, October 21, 2014; David Remnick, "Last of the Red Hots," *New Yorker*, September 18, 1995, 78: "He is also the only editor who, even in his sixties, made women blush and men straighten their posture."

72. Eugene Patterson, interview with David Halberstam, n.d., Halberstam Collection, box 194, folder 3, 1. These characterizations were confirmed in several interviews with the author.

73. Shelby Coffey, interview with the author, September 3, 2015.

74. Myra MacPherson, interview with the author, September 8, 2015.

75. Henry Allen, interview with the author, September 12, 2015.

76. Eugene Patterson, interview with Halberstam.

77. Bradlee was also very aggressive with hiring and firing. "With Graham's support, Bradlee was soon firing the lazy and the mediocre, the racist and the dull, and he then set about raiding topflight papers around the country for their best talent. The talent level in the newsroom began to shift, and so did the culture of the place." Remnick, "Citizen Kay," *The New Yorker*, January 20, 1997, 68.

78. See, for example, Rosenfeld, *From Kristallnacht to Watergate*, 113; Fallows, "Big Ben," 144.

79. John Anderson, interview with Halberstam.

80. Roberts, *Washington Post*, 379. Jeff Himmelman quoted Haynes Johnson as having said in October 2007, "[Bradlee] was determined to make the paper into what it could be: A great paper. Exciting. You had to read it. It was just, impact. He wanted impact. You ought to have impact, goddamnit. Instead of this namby-pamby stuff. And impact isn't cheap. It ought to have power, authority, and be well written; it ought to say something, and tell you about something you wanted to know; and it ought to be displayed so you don't miss it. That's what it's all about." Himmelman, *Yours in Truth*, 106.

81. Eugene Patterson, interview with Halberstam.

82. John Anderson, interview with Halberstam, n.d.

83. Ben Bagdikian, interview with David Halberstam, n.d., Halberstam Collection, box 192, folder 6, 14.

84. Larry Stern, interview with David Halberstam, n.d., Halberstam Collection, box 194, folder 9, n.p.

85. Roberts, *Washington Post*, 379.

86. Halberstam, *Powers That Be*, 540.

87. Myra MacPherson, interview with the author, September 8, 2015.

88. Bradlee, *A Good Life*, 300.

89. Thomas R. Schmidt, "Michael Kernan: Poet and Newspaperman," Presentation, IALJS 10, University of St. Thomas, Minneapolis, May 7–9, 2015.

90. Sally Quinn, *We Are Going to Make You a Star*.

91. Mills, *A Place in the News*, 169.

92. On the occasion of Bradlee's 49th birthday in 1970, they poured their criticism into a scathing satire. "Ben Bradlee, slim, attractive but complex executive editor of the Washington Post is 49 years old today but he doesn't look it. How does he manage to combine a successful career with the happy home life he has created in his gracious Georgetown home? In an interview today, pert, vivacious Mr. Bradlee revealed his secret. He relaxes after a day of whirlwind activity of the newspaper world by whomping [*sic*] up a batch of his favorite pecan-sauerbraten cookies for his thriving family. [. . .] What does Mrs. Bradlee think of her debonair husband's flair for journalism? 'I think it's great,' she said. 'Every wife should let her husband work. It makes him so well-rounded. Now he has something to talk about at the dinner table.' [. . .] Mr. Bradlee loves his work, but he is aware of the dangers involved. So far he does not feel he is in competition with his wife. 'When the day comes,' he said with a shudder, 'I'll know it's time to quit.' Mr. Bradlee's quick and easy recipe for pecan-sauerbraten cookies appears in tomorrow's bulletin." The New York Times Women's Caucus Papers, 1969–1986, 80-M169, folder 3, Schlesinger Library, Radcliffe Institute, Harvard University, Cambridge, MA.

93. Mills, *A Place in the News*, 169–70.

94. Donald A. Ritchie, *Reporting from Washington: The History of the Washington Press Corps*, 179.

95. Hollie West, interview with the author, May 4, 2016.

96. Memo from Thomas Kendrick to Elsie Carper, Eugene Patterson, and Ben Bradlee, February 16, 1970, Benjamin C. Bradlee Papers, box 47, folder 1.

97. Bradlee Papers, box 10.

98. Dorothy Gilliam, oral history interview with Donita Moorhus, C-Span, December 13, 1993, https://www.c-span.org/video/?299257-1/dorothy-gilliam-oral-history-interview.

99. Patterson included an extensive quote from Wicker: "First we must get the best people to work as journalists . . . good writers in the broadest literary sense . . . who in the best sense are the novelists of their time. The other thing we must do, having got all these good writers, we must create the kind of conditions in which they can do their best work. We can't do that by imposing formula writing, by group journalism. We are talking about artists." Eugene Patterson, memorandum to Ben Bradlee, June 1, 1971. See also, Wolfe, "The New Journalism," 1.

100. Memorandum from Eugene Patterson to Ben Bradlee, June 1, 1971, ECP. Emphasis added.

101. Memorandum from Richard Harwood to Bradlee and others, January 18, 1974, Bradlee Papers.

102. Sally Quinn, interview with the author, September 3, 2015.

103. Judy Bachrach, interview with the author, September 5, 2015.

104. Allen, interview with the author.

105. Allen, interview with the author.

106. Downie, interview with the author.

107. MacPherson, interview with the author.

108. Aaron Latham, "Waking Up with Sally Quinn," *New York*, July 16, 1973, 25.

109. Roberts, *Washington Post*, 468.

110. Memorandum from telephone desk to James Truitt, David Laventhol, Elsie Carper, Bradlee Papers, box 47, folder 1.

111. Helene Melzer, "Ben, Where Are You Hiding the Post Women's Section?" *Washingtonian*, April 1969, 53.

112. Dorothea Beall, "Governor's Bathroom," *Washington Post*, January 11, 1969, A12.

113. Andie Tucher, "Why Journalism History Matters: The Gaffe, the 'Stuff,' and the Historical Imagination," 433.

114. Paul du Gay, *Doing Cultural Studies: The Story of the Sony Walkman*, 85. Original emphasis.

115. Edith Fierst, "Woman's Point of View," Letters to the Editor, *Washington Post*, April 25, 1969, A26.

116. Letter from Mary L. Anderson (Mrs. Robert H. Anderson), April 30, 1969, Bradlee Papers, box 47, folder 1.

117. Letter from Martha Grosse to Editor of Style, January 10, 1969, Bradlee Papers, box 47, folder 1.

118. Margaret Borgers, "Flattered by Style," Letters to the Editor, *Washington Post*, April 30, 1969, A26.

119. Virginia T. Griffin, who had just moved from Massachusetts to Washington, wrote this "love letter" to Nicholas von Hoffman. Virginia T. Griffin, "Letter to the Editors," *Washington Post*, August 26, 1970.

120. Abrahamson, *Magazine-Made America*, 71. See also Lizabeth Cohen, *A Consumers' Republic: The Politics of Mass Consumption in Postwar America*.

121. In one story from 1977, for example, Kernan wrote about the boom of spiritual enlightenment. "And being American, they tackle the subject like . . . well they tackle the subject. With the zest of a gadget salesman, they descend upon the ancient philosophies of the East. Like tiger cubs they pummel and maul the Tai Chi Chuan, the yoga techniques, the Hindu practices that take the lifetime to master. They swarm to join classes, hear lectures, speed-read books that were a millennium in the writing." Michael Kernan, "Following the Master in Search of the Self," *Washington Post*, October 16, 1977.

122. Memorandum from Katharine Graham to Ben Bradlee and Eugene Patterson, May 6, 1969, ECP.

123. Memorandum from ECP to Harwood and Bradlee, October 6, 1970, ECP.

124. Memorandum from Eugene Patterson to Elsie Carper, July 1, 1970, ECP.

125. Davies, *Postwar Decline*, 127.

126. Memorandum from Eugene Patterson to Jim Daly, March 27, 1969, ECP.

127. *Washington Post* stockholder reports, 1972, 1979.

128. David L. Altheide, *Media Edge: Media Logic and Social Reality*, 9.

129. Altheide, *Media Edge*, 22.

130. Thomas Kendrick, memorandum to Howard Simons, October 15, 1973. Courtesy of Evelyn Small. Emphasis added.

131. Laura Longley Babb, ed., *Writing in Style: From the Style Section of the Washington Post: A New Perspective on the People and Trends of the Seventies.* In the introduction, Kendrick wrote: "One certainty is that the old feature formula of a grabber lead, a lively if unfocused anecdote or two, direct quotes and a good kicker was abruptly exposed as curiously obsolescent, unable to cope with the cultural change and revival of individualism that was rolling across the country. That tide rose so high and fast in the '60s that daily journalism often foundered in its task of forging patterns from the chaotic data spewing out of newsroom teletypes." Thomas R. Kendrick, "Introduction," ii.

132. Allen, interview with the author.

133. Remnick, "Last of the Red Hots," 80.

134. Fallows, "Big Ben," 53.

135. Fallows, "Big Ben," 144. See also Jeffrey Toobin, "The Regular Guy," *The New Yorker,* March 20, 2000, 99: "For more than a decade after Bradlee founded the section, in 1969, Style developed a distinctive voice—bitchy, funny, sometimes smugly fatuous, but always readable."

136. Fallows, "Big Ben," 144, 146.

137. Henry Allen, memorandum to Ben Bradlee, n.d. [ca. 1976], Bradlee Papers, box 43, folder 7.

138. Ben Bradlee, memorandum to Henry Allen, October 8, 1976, Bradlee Papers, box 43, folder 7.

139. Lee Hills, letter to Ben Bradlee and Eugene Patterson, May 20, 1977, Bradlee Papers, box 43, folder 7.

140. Pugwash transcript 1974, Bradlee Papers, box 41, folder 4.

141. Ben Bradlee, letter to Eugene Patterson and Lee Hills [with copies to the advisory board of the Pulitzer Prizes], November 9, 1977, Bradlee Papers, box 43, folder 7.

142. Today the wording is, "For distinguished feature writing giving prime consideration to quality of writing, originality and concision, using any available journalistic tool [. . .]." http://www.pulitzer.org/prize-winners-by-category/211.

143. Jack Limpert, "David Laventhol, Ben Bradlee, and the Rise and Fall of Style," *About Editing and Writing* (blog), jacklimpert.com, April 10, 2015, http://jacklimpert .com/2015/04/david-laventhol-rise-fall-style/.

144. See chapter 3.

145. Kendrick, "Introduction," v.

146. As one example, see Edwin Diamond, *Behind the Times: Inside the New New York Times.*

Chapter 3

1. Letter from Stuart Dim to Pete McKnight, August 5, 1977 [forwarded to Roy Peter Clark, August 24, 1977], ECP.

2. Associated Press Managing Editors Association, *The APME Red Book* 1975, 197.

3. Leo Bogart, *Press and Public: Who Reads What, When, Where, and Why in American Newspapers,* 1.

4. Thomas Winship, "Announcing: Annual ASNE Writing Awards." *Bulletin of the American Society of Newspaper Editors* 611 (December/January 1978): 12.

5. Michael Gartner, "What ASNE Is Doing to Help Find Out." *Bulletin of the American Society of Newspaper Editors* 606 (July/August 1977).

6. Elizabeth Bird and Robert W. Dardenne, "Myth, Chronicle, and Story: Exploring the Narrative Qualities of News," 76.

7. I am grateful to an anonymous reviewer who helped me clarify the specific characteristics of narrative journalism. He/she pointed out that "explanatory journalism is not necessarily narrative. And sociological topics for journalism are not necessarily presented in a narrative frame."

8. Explanatory journalism became a new category for the Pulitzer Prizes specifically to find a middle ground between traditional news reporting and narrative storytelling. According to a Wikipedia entry, "The Pulitzer Prize Board announced the new category in November 1984, citing a series of explanatory articles that seven months earlier had won the Pulitzer Prize for Feature Writing. The series, 'Making It Fly' by Peter Rinearson of The Seattle Times, was a 29,000-word account of the development of the Boeing 757 jetliner. It had been entered in the National Reporting category, but judges moved it to Feature Writing to award it a prize. In the aftermath, the Pulitzer Prize Board said it was creating the new category in part because of the ambiguity about where explanatory accounts such as 'Making It Fly' should be recognized. The Pulitzer Committee issues an official citation explaining the reasons for the award." Wikipedia. Accessed November 18, 2018, https://en.wikipedia.org/wiki/Pulitzer_Prize_for_Explanatory_Reporting. John Franklin, the first winner in this category also won the first Pulitzer Prize for Feature Writing in 1979. See references to Rinearson later in this chapter.

9. Thomas Hanitzsch and Tim P. Vos, "Journalism beyond Democracy: A New Look into Journalistic Roles in Political and Everyday Life," 158.

10. Karin Wahl-Jorgensen, "The Strategic Ritual of Emotionality: A Case Study of Pulitzer Prize-Winning Articles"; Frank Harbers and Marcel Broersma, "Between Engagement and Ironic Ambiguity: Mediating Subjectivity in Narrative Journalism"; Carolyn Kitch, "Tears and Trauma in the News," 29–39.

11. Vivien Lowndes and Mark Roberts, *Why Institutions Matter: The New Institutionalism in Political Science.*

12. Bruce Alan Williams and Michael X. Delli Carpini, *After Broadcast News: Media Regimes, Democracy, and the New Information Environment,* 16.

13. Richard L. Kaplan, "The News about New Institutionalism," 182.

14. Lowndes and Roberts, *Why Institutions Matter.*

15. Marc Schneiberg and Michael Lounsbury, "Social Movements and Institutional Analysis," 650.

16. Gaye Tuchman, *Making News: A Study in the Construction of Reality,* 179; see also Harvey Molotch and Marilyn Lester, "Accidental News: The Great Oil Spill as Local Occurrence and National Event"; Mark Fishman, *Manufacturing the News.*

17. As quoted in Timothy Leland, "Lilt and Lyricism on the News Pages," *Boston Globe,* May 12, 1978.

18. Letter from Eugene C. Patterson to Roy Peter Clark, January 24, 1977, ECP.

19. Letter from Eugene C. Patterson to Roy Peter Clark, March 14, 1977, ECP.

20. That same summer, the *Sacramento Bee* hosted Serrell Hillman, a professor at the University of Hawaii, for three months to tutor reporters about writing. But there was no follow-up and this project did not receive any attention later on. It was only mentioned in a letter between ASNE board editors. Letter from Michael Gartner to Michael O'Neill on October 11, 1977, ECP.

21. Associated Press Managing Editors Association, *The APME Red Book 1977*, 2.

22. Robert Darnton, "Writing News and Telling Stories," 186.

23. *Times-O-Gram*, vol. 27, no. 6, August 5, 1977.

24. *Times-O-Gram*, vol. 27, no. 6, August 5, 1977.

25. Roy Peter Clark, "Infectious Cronkitis," *New York Times*, March 24, 1975, 31.

26. Roy Peter Clark. Conversation with the author.

27. American Society of Newspaper Editors. Convention. *Problems of Journalism: Proceedings of the 1978 Convention, American Society of Newspaper Editors*, 1978, 176.

28. Fishman, *Manufacturing the News*; Herbert J. Gans, *Deciding What's News: A Study of CBS Evening News, NBC Nightly News, Newsweek, and Time*; Michael Schudson, *Discovering the News: A Social History of American Newspapers*; Michael Schudson, *The Sociology of News*; Tuchman, *Making News*.

29. Schudson, *Discovering the News*; Hazel Dicken-Garcia, *Journalistic Standards in Nineteenth-century America*.

30. The most prominent examples were *Esquire*, *New York*, and *Rolling Stone*.

31. American Society of Newspaper Editors. Convention. *Problems of Journalism: Proceedings of the 1978 Convention, American Society of Newspaper Editors*, 1978, 177.

32. American Society of Newspaper Editors. Convention. *Problems of Journalism: Proceedings of the 1978 Convention, American Society of Newspaper Editors*, 1978, 176–77.

33. Barbie Zelizer, *Taking Journalism Seriously: News and the Academy*.

34. As quoted in Paul Alfred Pratte, *Gods within the Machine: A History of the American Society of Newspaper Editors, 1923–1993*, x. The "Brahmins" quote is from Everett Dennis.

35. Michael O'Neill, "What ASNE Is Doing to Help Find Out," *Bulletin of the American Society of Newspaper Editors* 606 (July/August 1977): 12.

36. Former APME president Lee Hills as quoted in North Central Publishing Company, *Fifty and Feisty: APME, 1933 to 1983*, 33.

37. Associated Press Managing Editors Association, *The APME Red Book 1977*, 147.

38. James Ragdale (Editor of the *New Bedford* [MA] *Standard-Time*), *Bulletin of the American Society of Newspaper Editors* 625 (July/August, 1979): 6–7.

39. Quoted in Thomas Winship, "Announcing: Annual ASNE Writing Awards," *Bulletin of the American Society of Newspaper Editors* 611 (December/January 1978): 12. Emphasis added.

40. See Pratte, *Gods Within the Machine*, 129–33.

41. Leo Bogart, *Preserving the Press: How Daily Newspapers Mobilized to Keep Their Readers.*

42. American Society of Newspaper Editors. Convention. *Problems of Journalism: Proceedings of the 1978 Convention, American Society of Newspaper Editors,* 1978, 87–88.

43. American Society of Newspaper Editors. Convention. *Problems of Journalism: Proceedings of the 1978 Convention, American Society of Newspaper Editors,* 1978, 175.

44. American Society of Newspaper Editors. Convention. *Problems of Journalism: Proceedings of the 1980 Convention, American Society of Newspaper Editors,* 1980, 111. See also *The Editors' Exchange* 2, no. 1 (January 1979), ECP.

45. David Shaw, "Smoothing Out the First Rough Draft of History," 28. I did not find any explanation of why newspapers in the mid-range of circulation were most eager to organize seminars. It seems probable that bigger papers ran their own trainings while smaller papers lacked the funding.

46. For instance, the first committee included editors from the following newspapers: *Washington Post, Wall Street Journal,* Knight-Ridder newspapers, *Los Angeles Times, Chicago Tribune* and *Chicago Sun-Times, Boston Globe, New Britain (CT) Herald, Greenwood (MS) Commonwealth, Raleigh (NC) News and Observer, Anchorage Daily News.* Originally, there were four categories (news/deadline, news/nondeadline, features, and commentary), but that changed throughout the years.

47. Alessandro Portelli, "The Peculiarities of Oral History," 100.

48. See examples from these interviews below after the Janet Cooke section.

49. *The Editors' Exchange* 2, no. 1 (January 1979), ECP.

50. *The Editors' Exchange* 2, no. 10 (October 1979), ECP.

51. *The Editors' Exchange* 2, no. 12 (December 1979), ECP.

52. Associated Press Managing Editors Association, *The APME Red Book 1979,* 43–44.

53. *The Editors' Exchange* 4, no. 2 (February 1981), ECP. The *Tallahassee Democrat* also created the position of an assistant managing editor of writing. See Roy Peter Clark, ed., *Best Newspaper Writing 1982,* xii.

54. Associated Press Media Editors, Writing and Editing Report, Tulsa, Oklahoma, Oct. 16–19, 1979. Associated Press Media Editors, *How do we write? The Problem . . . The Treatment . . . The Training: A Report by the Writing and Editing Committee* (San Diego, California, November 9–12, 1982), ECP; American Society of Newspaper Editors. Convention. *ASNE: Proceedings of the 1982 Convention of the American Society of Newspaper Editors,* 1982, 30–32; *The Editors' Exchange* 5, no. 7 (August 1982), ECP; *The Editors' Exchange* 7, no. 2 (February 1984), ECP; *The Editors' Exchange* 7, no. 2 (February 1984), ECP.

55. For instance, the Southern Newspaper Publishers Association Foundation at seminars in 1978 in Charlotte, North Carolina, and El Paso, Texas. *The Editors' Exchange* 2, no. 1 (January 1979), ECP.

56. "So we hear the call for good writing from editors all over the country. We hear it at the *Minneapolis Tribune,* where at the insistence of the staff, English teacher Dave Wood was brought to work with the writers. We hear it at *The Christian Science*

Monitor, where Lucille De View is working with young writers; at the *Honolulu Advertiser,* where Roger Tatarian worked with the staff; at the *Reading (PA) Eagle and Times,* where Lawrence Suhre helped beef up the skills of copy editors; at the *Orlando Sentinel Star,* where June Smith recently turned writing coach; at the *Anderson (S.C.) Daily Mail,* where Mark Etheridge undertook a summer's writing project. The writing coach has become a new profession. The *Boston Globe* has a fine one, Don Murray. And the *Globe* may soon create a position called the Writing Editor. [. . .] Seminars and workshops have popped up everywhere. Joe Ungaro has set up a series of workshops with guest speakers for the staff of the Westchester-Rockland Newspapers; API will hold its third seminar devoted exclusively to writing and editing this July; SNPA will have another one next week." American Society of Newspaper Editors. Convention. *Problems of Journalism: Proceedings of the 1980 Convention, American Society of Newspaper Editors,* 1980, 115.

57. American Society of Newspaper Editors. Convention. *Problems of Journalism: Proceedings of the 1980 Convention, American Society of Newspaper Editors,* 1980, 118.

58. Cooke had done a lot of reporting on the drug problem in Washington, DC, and had talked to a variety of social workers, city officials, and drug rehabilitation researchers. But as she was quoted after the scandal broke, "It was a fabrication. I did so much work on it, but it's a composite." Bill Green, "The Confession," *Washington Post,* April 19, 1981. Doubts about Cooke's veracity were first raised by former editors who read her biographical information. Further investigations showed that she had made up her academic credentials. When confronted with these findings, Cooke confessed the fabrication of the article.

59. In many ways, my analysis parallels the conclusions of David Eason's influential study "On Journalistic Authority." See David L. Eason, "On Journalistic Authority: The Janet Cooke Scandal," 431. Yet, whereas Eason looked at the case through the lens of journalistic authority, my interest lies in examining the functions of narrative reporting and writing. Eason actually did not see any narrative value in Cooke's story: "The story," he wrote, "designed to draw attention to the heroin problem in the city, was formally an unexceptional human interest story."

60. Martha S. Stewart, "Letter to the Editor," *Washington Post,* October 4, 1980.

61. Sharron Jackson, "Letter to the Editor," *Washington Post,* October 4, 1980.

62. "Capital Offense," *Wall Street Journal,* April 17, 1981.

63. Jonathan Friendly, "Falsification of Prize Article Puts a Spotlight on How Newspapers Check," *New York Times,* April 17, 1981.

64. Letter to the Editor, *Washington Post,* April 18, 1981

65. Editorial, "New Look on New Journalism," *Washington Star,* April 21, 1981.

66. "Exploring Jimmy's World," 28.

67. Penn Kimball, "A Multiple Embarrassment," 34.

68. Jonathan Friendly, "Disclosure of Two Fabricated Articles Causes Papers to Re-Examine Their Rules," *New York Times,* May 25, 1981.

69. Joseph W. Shoquist, "A Hard Line for Hard News," *Bulletin of the American Society of Newspaper Editors* 634 (July/August 1980): 11.

70. David Shaw, "Smoothing Out," 28.

71. Clark, *Best Newspaper Writing 1982*, xvi. He continued, "We do not stand for self-indulgent overwriting, deceptive leads, the enforcement of stereotypes or those techniques properly in the domain of fiction: composite characters, improved quotations, rearranged facts, invented authorial presence or the omniscient looking into minds."

72. Clark, *Best Newspaper Writing 1982*, xvii.

73. The following analysis is based on interviews from the first ten volumes of *Best Newspaper Writing* that were published between 1979 and 1988. In lieu of a standardized coding scheme, I conducted an applied cultural analysis as conceptualized by Driskill and Brenton. They suggest a specific analytical frame to identify "how organization members create values, norms, and metaphors." Gerald W. Driskill and Angela Laird Brenton, *Organizational Culture in Action: A Cultural Analysis Workbook*, 19. As a result, I identified particular clusters of descriptions and metaphors, allowing me to draw conclusions about the emergence and expansion of norms, values, and beliefs with regard to narrative journalism.

74. Clark, *Best Newspaper Writing 1979*, 118.

75. Clark, *Best Newspaper Writing 1979*, 118.

76. Clark, *Best Newspaper Writing 1980*, 116. The introduction to McCabe's interview said: "Skillful journalists are experimenting with a type of reporting that goes well beyond the traditional 'human interest' story. Some are calling it 'people journalism,' but it should not be confused with the journalism of gossip and glamor, practiced more and more to attract readers to newspapers. Reporters are centering their stories not only on the council meeting, the court decision or the administrative memo, but also on the people directly affected by public policy, the men and women and children who suffer from bad decisions regarding inflation, taxes or energy. No one practices that type of journalism with more skill and dedication than Carol McCabe [. . .]." Ibid., 65.

77. Clark, *Best Newspaper Writing 1980*, 61.

78. The role of emotions in fieldwork for research is of particular importance to qualitative researchers. See Sherryl Kleinman and Martha A. Copp, *Emotions and Fieldwork*.

79. Clark, *Best Newspaper Writing 1984*, 100.

80. Clark, *Best Newspaper Writing 1980*, 118.

81. Clark, *Best Newspaper Writing 1981*, 30.

82. Clark, *Best Newspaper Writing 1980*, 37. William E. Blundell, *The Art and Craft of Feature Writing: Based on the Wall Street Journal Guide*. See also a comment by James Kindall: "Even people who reveal their motivation, it takes an analysis on your part whether that's true or not. That's the difficult part. You have to tie up everything in one large package and see what you have. That's always risky. I'm always queasy about it." Clark, *Best Newspaper Writing 1984*, 102.

83. Clark, *Best Newspaper Writing 1981*, 73–74. See also a comment by Carol McCabe: "I'm writing stories. I'm using them as characters in stories. They're telling their own stories. They come to life because they are alive, and I try to employ

language skillfully so they are not just pieces of type. Most of us are into working with characters in the same way that fiction writers do." Clark, *Best Newspaper Writing 1980*, 115.

84. Clark, *Best Newspaper Writing 1984*, 238.

85. Clark, *Best Newspaper Writing 1984*, 215.

86. Clark, *Best Newspaper Writing 1984*, 47.

87. E.g., Jon Franklin, *Writing for Story: Craft Secrets of Dramatic Nonfiction by a Two-Time Pulitzer Prize-Winner*; Blundell, *Art and Craft*.

88. Helen MacGill Hughes, cited in Judy Polumbaum, "Human Interest Journalism," 730.

89. For discussions of tabloidization, see Colin Sparks and John Tulloch, *Tabloid Tales: Global Debates over Media Standards* as well as S. Elizabeth Bird, "Tabloidization: What It Is, and Does It Really Matter?" 40–50.

90. See also Karin Wahl-Jorgensen and Thomas R. Schmidt, "News and Storytelling."

91. *1988 APME Writing and Editing Committee Report*, ECP.

92. Steven Lovelady, "How This Lede Worked," *Bulletin of the American Society of Newspaper Editors* 627 (October 1979), 4.

93. Associated Press Managing Editors Association, *APME Writing and Editing Committee Report 1988*, 25. Associated Press Managing Editors Association records, Wisconsin Historical Society.

94. *APME Writing and Editing Committee Report 1988*, 30.

95. *APME Writing and Editing Committee Report 1988*, 5.

96. *APME Writing and Editing Committee Report 1988*, 7.

97. *APME Writing and Editing Committee Report 1988*, 31.

98. *APME Writing and Editing Committee Report 1988*, 29.

99. American Society of Newspaper Editors. Convention. *ASNE: Proceedings of the 1983 Convention, American Society of Newspaper Editors*, 1983.

100. In 1985, for example, *Editors' Exchange* featured initiatives in the following newsrooms: *Watertown (NY) Daily Times*; *Lawrence (MA) Eagle-Tribune*; *Dallas Morning News*; *Milwaukee Journal*; *Shreveport (LA) Times*; *Detroit Free Press*; Salt Lake City's *Deseret News*. See *The Editors' Exchange* 8, no. 1 (January 1985); *The Editors' Exchange* 8, no. 2 (February 1985); *The Editors' Exchange* 8, no. 6 (August 1985).

101. Arnold Rosenfeld of the *Austin (TX) American-Statesman* said, "Dr. Clark has become perhaps the foremost expert on good, and, conversely, bad newspaper writing." American Society of Newspaper Editors. Convention. *ASNE: Proceedings of the 1985 Convention, American Society of Newspaper Editors*, 1985, 213.

102. American Society of Newspaper Editors. Convention. *ASNE: Proceedings of the 1987 Convention, American Society of Newspaper Editors*, 1987, 230. For a study about the impact of writing coaches, see Ray Laakaniemi, "An Analysis of Writing Coach Programs on American Daily Newspapers," 569–75.

103. *Report of the APME Writing and Editing Committee, Toronto, Canada, October 20–23, 1981*, 11. Associated Press Managing Editors Association records, Wisconsin Historical Society.

104. Associated Press Managing Editors Association, *The APME Red Book 1984*. Associated Press Managing Editors Association records, Wisconsin Historical Society.

105. Wahl-Jorgensen, "Strategic Ritual," 130.

106. Wahl-Jorgensen, "Strategic Ritual," 130.

107. David Herman, *The Cambridge Companion to Narrative*, 9.

108. John J. Pauly, "The Politics of the New Journalism," 123.

Chapter 4

1. William Glaberson, "James K. Batten, 59, Knight-Ridder Chairman," *New York Times*, June 26, 1995, B8.

2. James K. Batten, "Too Many Newspaper People Continue to Ignore Important Realities of Modern Life—and Modern Readers," *Bulletin of the American Society of Newspaper Editors* (May/June 1989): 18–21, 20.

3. Batten, "Too Many Newspaper People," 21.

4. Batten became a champion for the public journalism movement whose proponents also challenged traditional notions of journalism albeit with more emphasis toward notions of participation and public accountability. See Edmund B. Lambeth, Philip E. Meyer, and Esther Thorson, eds., *Assessing Public Journalism*; Don H. Corrigan, *The Public Journalism Movement in America: Evangelists in the Newsroom*.

5. Anthony M. Nadler, *Making the News Popular: Mobilizing U.S. News Audiences*.

6. "US 'narrative' journalism," Rodney Benson argued, "as a form of serious (or light) entertainment, emerge[d] in the context of advertiser pressures to attract the largest possible (high-consuming) audiences." Rodney Benson, "On the Explanatory and Political Uses of Journalism History," 9.

7. American Newspaper Publishers Association, *90 Facts about Newspapers*, April 1990.

8. At the ANPA convention in Los Angeles, journalism professor Gerald Stone was invited to present a study on teenage and young adult readership. "Things have not gotten better since 1980," Stone told about fifty executives and journalism academics. "If anything, the most foreboding prognoses of the early 1970s have come to pass. When we lose our young readers, we are faced with a serious, and potentially disastrous, threat to the newspaper industry's future." Quoted in Mark Fitzgerald, "A Year of Retrenchment: Newspaper Industry Wonders about Its Future as a Second Straight Year of Economic Downturn Comes to a Close," *Editor & Publisher* 124, no. 1 (Jan. 5, 1991): 9.

9. Joseph Turow, *Breaking up America: Advertisers and the New Media World*, 31.

10. American Society of Newspaper Editors. Convention. *ASNE: Proceedings of the 1988 Convention of the American Society of Newspaper Editors*, 1988, 231.

11. Thomas C. Leonard, *News for All: America's Coming-of-Age with the Press*.

12. James L. Baughman, *The Republic of Mass Culture: Journalism, Filmmaking, and Broadcasting in America since 1941*, 189.

13. Quoted in David Nimmer, "Reinventing Newspapers: Here We Go Again," *Bulletin of the American Society of Newspaper Editors* (October 1993), 9.

14. American Society of Newspaper Editors. Convention. "What We Learned from ASNE's Potential Readers Study," *ASNE: Proceedings of the 1985 Convention, American Society of Newspaper Editors,* 1995.

15. Doug Underwood, *When MBAs Rule the Newsroom: How the Marketers and Managers are Reshaping Today's Media.*

16. Doug Underwood, "When MBAs Rule the Newsroom," *Columbia Journalism Review* (March/April 1988), 23.

17. Consider this example from Ryfe: "From the 1930s to the 1970s, when journalists enjoyed their greatest autonomy from commercial pressures, hard news dominated the front pages of most newspapers around the country. But, as journalists sought to give readers more of what they wanted in the news, softer news followed." David M. Ryfe, *Can Journalism Survive?: An Inside Look at American Newsrooms,* 43.

18. Christopher P. Wilson, *The Labor of Words: Literary Professionalism in the Progressive Era,* xiv.

19. Debra Gersh, "Inverted Pyramid Turned Upside Down," *Editor & Publisher,* May 1, 1993, 22.

20. Larry Beaupre, "Features Grow Up," *Report of the Features Committee,* APME 1987, 1.

21. Pamela Bruger Scott: "'Lifestyle' Moves from Coping to Quality," *Report of the Features Committee,* APME 1987, 2.

22. As quoted in Susan Love, "From 'Women's Pages' to 'Style Sections' to—What? Feature Editors Wrestle over the Best Way to Gather Wandering Readers," *Bulletin of the American Society of Newspaper Editors* (February 1995), 5.

23. Warren Watson, "Narrative Style Adds Life to Your Pages," *American Editor* (March/April 1999): 9.

24. American Society of Newspaper Editors, *ASNE: Proceedings of the 1992 Convention of the American Society of Newspaper Editors,* 294.

25. American Society of Newspaper Editors, *ASNE: Proceedings of the 1994 Convention of the American Society of Newspaper Editors,* 261.

26. American Society of Newspaper Editors, *ASNE: Proceedings of the 1989 Convention of the American Society of Newspaper Editors,* 307.

27. *The Bulletin of the American Society of Newspaper Editors* (April 1991), 30–31.

28. American Society of Newspaper Editors, *ASNE: Proceedings of the 1991 Convention of the American Society of Newspaper Editors,* 219.

29. Thomas Maier, *Newhouse: All the Glitter, Power, and Glory of America's Richest Media Empire and the Secretive Man Behind It,* 354–55, 358.

30. Brent Cunningham, "The Newhouse Way," 24.

31. Linda Fibich, "A Brand New Ballgame," 28.

32. Sandra Mims Rowe, interview with the author, February 9, 2017.

33. "Sandra Mims Rowe: She Just Wins."

34. Rowe, interview with the author.

35. Jack Hart, interview with the author, October 18, 2016.

36. Hart, interview with the author.

37. The collected newsletters are part of the Oregonian Publishing Company Records, 1855–2008, located at the Oregon Historical Society in Portland, Oregon.

38. *Second Takes* 1, no. 1 (May 1989): 1.

39. *Second Takes* 1, no. 5 (September 1989): 4.

40. *Second Takes* 1, no. 9 (January 1990): 3. He continued, "That's not the sort of companion most of us would want to take along for a relaxing spell in an easy chair. It's not the kind of personality likely to attract the young readers we urgently need. And it's not the style that suits the informal ways typical of life here in the Pacific Northwest."

41. *Second Takes* 1, no. 9 (January 1990): 6.

42. *Second Takes* 1, no. 10 (February 1990): 1, 8.

43. *Second Takes* 2, no. 2 (June 1990): 1.

44. *Second Takes* 2, no. 2 (June 1990): 5.

45. *Second Takes* 2, no. 2 (June 1990): 5.

46. Jim Camin, "How the *Oregonian* Stacked Up at API," *Second Takes* 1, no. 11 (March 1990): 5.

47. Report by the APME Writing and Editing Committee, 1987, ECB.

48. *Second Takes* 2, no. 4 (August 1990): 1.

49. *Second Takes* 3, no. 4 (August 1991): 3.

50. *Second Takes* 3, no. 4 (August 1991): 8. "For one thing, experienced journalists sometimes reject the literary approach because it lacks an obvious news hook. Good stories may be about nobodies, at least in the sense that their principal players hold no public offices, have nothing to do with public policy issues and haven't been near the center of any major news events. Good stories also are timeless, and so they may lack the immediacy that conforms to the conventional definition of news. And because they teach broad truths, true stories seldom display the news-you-can-use practicality of more conventional lifestyle features."

51. Fibich, "Brand New Ballgame," 28.

52. Rowe, interview with the author.

53. *Second Takes* 5, no. 5 (September 1993): 1.

54. *Second Takes* 5, no. 5 (September 1993): 4.

55. *Second Takes* 5, no. 6 (October 1993): 1.

56. I am thankful to Christopher Wilson for sharing this thought.

57. *Second Takes* 6, no. 2 (June 1994): 1.

58. *Second Takes* 6, no. 2 (June 1994): 1.

59. Rowe, interview with the author.

60. Tom Hallman's story "Life of a Salesman" was a finalist in the nondeadline category.

61. *Second Takes* 8, no. 7 (November 1996): 1.

62. *Second Takes* 8, no. 8 (December 1996): 1.

63. *Second Takes* 8, no. 12 (April 1997): 1.

64. *Second Takes* 9, no. 9 (January 1998): 1.

65. *Second Takes* 9, no. 9 (January 1998): 2.

66. Robin Pogrebin, "Boston Columnist Is Ousted for Fabricated Articles," *New York Times*, June 19, 1998, http://www.nytimes.com/1998/06/19/us/boston-columnist-is-ousted-for-fabricated-articles.html.

67. *Second Takes* 11, no. 2 (July 1998). For number 6, see also: "However, [one participant] voiced caution about surrendering the narrative to the character's viewpoint. 'You have to be fair to your readers, too,' he said. If the writer allows sources to sanitize the material excessively, 'you end up with a dry story and a false impression.'"

68. *Second Takes* 9, no. 10 (February 1998): 5.

69. *Second Takes* 9, no. 10 (February 1998): 8.

70. "The Oregonian and the Pulitzer Prize," April 8, 2013, http://www.oregonlive.com /editors/index.ssf/2013/04/the_oregonian_and_the_pulitzer.html. See also Rowe's perspective: "These two series [Hallman, INS] are very different—completely different subjects of course, calling for differing reporting methods, story structures and writing styles. One a serial written by a master of the journalistic narrative form, the other an exhaustively reported explanatory story with an investigative edge that shed light on an issue of complexity in a way only a newspaper can or will do. They had a lot in common, too. Both got to the heart of their subject matter and adhered to the highest journalistic standards." Sandra Mims Rowe, "Why Series Matter."

71. Mark Lisheron, "Riding High," 34; "10 That Do It Right."

72. "Editors of the Year 2008: Sandy Rowe & Peter Bhatia," *Editor & Publisher*, Feb. 1, 2008.

73. Winnie Hu, "The Training Track."

74. *Workbench* 1995, The Poynter Institute.

75. Roy Peter Clark, "A Few Tools from . . .," *American Editor* (October/November 1998).

76. Manuscript "National Writers Workshop," n.d. [probably 1996 or 1997], The Poynter Institute, 2.

77. Manuscript "National Writers Workshop," 3.

78. Chris Harvey, "Tom Wolfe's Revenge."

79. American Society of Newspaper Editors. Convention. *Problems of Journalism: Proceedings of the 1990 Convention of the American Society of Newspaper Editors*, 1990, 205.

80. Sandra Mims Rowe, "Awarding Good Writing: A Happy ASNE Mission," *American Editor* (March 1998), 2.

81. Roy Peter Clark and Christopher Scanlan, eds., *America's Best Newspaper Writing: A Collection of ASNE Prizewinners*, iii.

82. For example, Walt Harrington, *Intimate Journalism: The Art and Craft of Reporting Everyday Life*; Lee Gutkind, *The Art of Creative Nonfiction: Writing and Selling the Literature of Reality*.

83. "Can Good Storytelling Save Newspapers?" (Fisher Auditorium, October, 21, 1998. University Archives, University of Missouri), video tape (VHS), accessed February 9, 2017, http://muarchives.missouri.edu/c20-13-1_box_list.html.

84. Warren Watson, "Narrative Style Adds Life to Your Pages," *American Editor* (March/April 1999): 9, 11.

85. *Nieman Reports*, Spring 2002, 58.

86. Jacqui Banaszynksi, interview with the author, February 2, 2017.

87. Mark Kramer, "Narrative Journalism Comes of Age," 5.

88. Kramer, "Narrative Journalism Comes of Age," 5.

89. Madeleine Blais, "Literary Nonfiction Constructs a Narrative Foundation." 42.

90. William F. Woo, "Just Write What Happened," 16.

91. Nieman Foundation, "Talking about Narrative Journalism," 20.

92. Jacqui Banaszynski, "Why We Need Stories." 42.

93. Verica Rupar, *Journalism and Meaning-Making: Reading the Newspaper*.

94. Kevin G. Barnhurst and John Nerone, *The Form of News*.

95. Marcel Broersma, *Form and Style in Journalism: European Newspapers and the Presentation of News, 1880–2005*, 20.

96. James L. Baughman, "Wounded but Not Slain: The Orderly Retreat of the American Newspaper," 123.

97. John H. McManus, "The Commercialization of News," 219.

98. See the examples of the *Baltimore Sun* and the *Providence Journal* above. The *Bulletin* regularly featured reports of narrative and explanatory success stories. For example, the cover story in the April 1993 issue was "The Long Story: Readers Will Go to Any Length If the Story Interests Them," *Bulletin of the American Society of Newspaper Editors* (April 1993).

99. American Society of Newspaper Editors. Convention. *Problems of Journalism: Proceedings of the 2001 Convention of the American Society of Newspaper Editors*, 2001, 55.

100. American Society of Newspaper Editors, *Problems of Journalism*, 55.

101. Daly, *Covering America*, ix.

102. Picard, "Twilight or New Dawn of Journalism?," 501.

Chapter 5

1. Rodney Benson, *Shaping Immigration News: A French-American Comparison*; Kevin G. Barnhurst and Diana Mutz, "American Journalism and the Decline in Event-Centered Reporting," 27–53; Pablo J. Boczkowski and Eugenia Mitchelstein, *The News Gap: When the Information Preferences of the Media and the Public Diverge*; Katharine Fink and Michael Schudson, "The Rise of Contextual Journalism, 1950s–2000s," 3–20; Michele Weldon, *Everyman News: The Changing American Front Page*; Thomas E. Patterson, *Out of Order*.

2. Fink and Schudson, "Rise of Contextual Journalism."

3. Fink and Schudson, "Rise of Contextual Journalism," 9.

4. "Such stories encourage readers to be interested in, have compassion for, or empathize with, the experiences and problems of people who are largely unfamiliar to them. Social empathy stories often use personal experiences to highlight larger social problems [. . .]." Fink and Schudson, "Rise of Contextual Journalism," 9.

5. Fink and Schudson, "Rise of Contextual Journalism," 12.

6. Benson, *Shaping Immigration News*, 88–89.

7. Weldon defined a feature as "a story not tied to a specific event on the previous day. Timeliness is not the main news hook. It can be a profile, trend story, enterprise piece, investigative piece, round-up, analysis, travel piece, review, commentary,

anniversary story, or exclusive. It is not deadline-driven. A feature piece has human interest but may not have many of the crucial elements of newsworthiness: timeliness, prominence, proximity, unusualness, diversity, consequence, or impact." Weldon, *Everyman News*, 34.

8. Barnhurst and Mutz, "American Journalism," 44. See also: "In their effort to provide context and interpretation, journalists identified individuals less often by name and more often by demographic group. Fewer ordinary people played roles as actors and victims, replaced by a cast of official sources, outside experts, and commentators. The number of current events went down in these longer stories. References to history and temporal change went up. The index of location also grew, as journalists abandoned the particular street address in favor of broader geographical frames of reference." Barnhurst and Mutz, "American Journalism," 40.

9. Carl Sessions Stepp, "The State of the American Newspaper: Then and Now," 60.

10. Gaye Tuchman, *Making News: A Study in the Construction of Reality*; Benson, *Shaping Immigration News*.

11. Jesper Strömbäck and Susana Salgado, "Interpretive Journalism: A Review of Concepts, Operationalizations and Key Findings," 147.

12. See the discussion from the Nieman conference above, especially the contribution from Jacqui Banaszynski on page 134.

13. My discussion of institutional theory is limited to its proponents within the field of journalism studies and does not extend to a wide range of sociological approaches. See for example Greenwood, Oliver, Sahlin, and Suddaby, eds., *The Sage Handbook of Organizational Institutionalism*.

14. James G. March and Johan P. Olsen, *Rediscovering Institutions: The Organizational Basis of Politics*, 3. Original emphasis.

15. Tim Cook, *Governing with the News: The News Media as a Political Institution*; Bartholomew H. Sparrow, *Uncertain Guardians: The News Media as a Political Institution*; Richard L. Kaplan, *Politics and the American Press: The Rise of Objectivity, 1865–1920*; David M. Ryfe, *Can Journalism Survive?: An Inside Look at American Newsrooms*.

16. Cook, *Governing with the News*, 234.

17. Ryfe, "Introduction," 135–44.

18. Tim Cook, "The News Media as Political Institution: Looking Backward and Looking Forward," 165.

19. Jefferson Pooley, *James W. Carey and Communication Research: Reputation at the University's Margins*.

20. James W. Carey, "A Cultural Approach to Communication," 70.

21. Carey, "Communications and Economics," 64.

22. Carey, "Mass Communication and Cultural Studies," 199.

23. Carey, "Mass Communication," 43.

24. James W. Carey and Lawrence Grossberg, "From New England to Illinois: The Invention of (American) Cultural Studies," 199.

25. Carolyn Kitch, "A News of Feeling as Well as Fact: Mourning and Memorial in American Newsmagazines."

26. Barbie Zelizer, *Taking Journalism Seriously: News and the Academy*, 176.

27. Michael Schudson, *The Sociology of News*, 26.

28. Schudson, *Sociology of News*, 25.

29. Zelizer, *Taking Journalism Seriously*, 78.

30. Christopher P. Wilson, *The Labor of Words: Literary Professionalism in the Progressive Era*, xii.

31. Wilson, *Labor of Words*, xiv. Original emphasis.

32. Peter Burke, *History and Social Theory*, 27.

33. Thomas Bernard Connery, *Journalism and Realism: Rendering American Life*.

34. Jack Hart, *Second Takes* 1, no. 1 (May 1989): 1.

35. Tom Wicker, "The Greening of the Press," 12.

36. Michael Schudson said as much when he wrote, "All news stories are stories, but some are more storylike than others." Schudson, *Sociology of News*, 191–92. Nevertheless, some scholars have taken Schudson's analytical point for a conceptual one, conflating storytelling with sensationalism. "Newspapers that stress their storytelling function seek to create for readers 'satisfying aesthetic experiences which help them to interpret their own lives and to relate them to the nation, town, or class to which they belong.' They follow the market and try to please their readers and advertisers. Usually these newspapers are labeled as popular or sensationalist. They tend to use an emotionally-involving style, often characterized as sensationalism, that aims to appeal to the emotions of their readers." Marcel Broersma, *Form and Style in Journalism: European Newspapers and the Presentation of News, 1880–2005*, xvi.

37. Arthur W. Frank, *Letting Stories Breathe: A Socio-Narratology*, 2.

38. Tenenboim-Weinblatt observed, "Interestingly, while journalists refer to news as *stories*, they tend to vehemently reject the suggestion that they themselves are storytellers or that their stories are anything but a reflection of reality." Tenenboim-Weinblatt, "News as Narrative," 954. See also Zelizer, *Taking Journalism Seriously*, 176–78.

39. See for example, Mark Kramer, "Breakable Rules for Literary Journalists," Nieman Storyboard, January 1, 2015. Retrieved from: http://niemanstoryboard.org/stories/breakable-rules-for-literary-journalists/.

40. George Getschow, "Introduction: The Best American Newspaper Narratives of 2012," 1–12.

41. Carolyn Kitch, "Tears and Trauma in the News," 36.

42. Jama Lazerow, "1960–1974," 91.

43. Schudson, *The Rise of the Right To Know: Politics and the Culture of Transparency, 1945–1975*.

44. Robert O. Self, *All in the Family: The Realignment of American Democracy since the 1960s*.

45. Lizabeth Cohen, *A Consumers' Republic: The Politics of Mass Consumption in Postwar America*.; Sarah E. Igo, *The Averaged American: Surveys, Citizens, and the Making of a Mass Public*; Juliet Schor, *The Overspent American: Upscaling, Downshifting, and the New Consumer*.

46. Benson, *Shaping Immigration News*; Ryfe, *Can Journalism Survive?*; Lance W. Bennett, *News: The Politics of Illusion*.

47. G. Stuart Adam, *Notes Towards a Definition of Journalism: Understanding an Old Craft as an Art Form*, 24–25.

48. See, for example, Ferree, Gamson, Gerhards, and Rucht, eds., *Shaping Abortion Discourse: Democracy and the Public Sphere in Germany and the United States*, 228. "Rather than dialogue and formal argumentation, constructionists particularly value narrative as a characteristic of content and style that challenges both the diffuse power relations of daily life and the concentrated power of disembodied formal political institutions by revealing the connections between them. Legitimating the language of the lifeworld in discourse privileges the experiential knowledge of ordinary citizens and contributes to their empowerment. Finally, closure after a decision is suspect since it can so easily suppress the diversity of expression that vitalizes democracy."

49. Benson, *Shaping Immigration News*, 48.

Appendix: Methodology

1. MaryAnn Yodelis Smith, "The Method of History," 316–30.

2. John Scott, *A Matter of Record: Documentary Sources in Social Research*.

3. Lindsay Prior, *Using Documents in Social Research*, 4.

4. Dustin Harp, "Newspapers' Transition from Women's to Style Pages," 203. For the value of studying the trade press, see also Joseph Turow, *Breaking up America: Advertisers and the New Media World*.

5. Gerald W. Driskill and Angela Laird Brenton, *Organizational Culture in Action: A Cultural Analysis Workbook*, 19.

6. Bradley T. Erford, *Research and Evaluation in Counseling*, 102.

7. Clifford Geertz, *The Interpretation of Cultures: Selected Essays*.

8. Thomas J. Sugrue, *Origins of the Urban Crisis: Race and Inequality in Postwar Detroit*, 11.

Bibliography

Archival Sources

Associated Press Managing Editors Association Records, 1935–2005. Wisconsin Historical Society.

Bradlee, Benjamin C. Papers. The Harry Ransom Center. University of Texas at Austin.

Clark, Roy Peter. Personal Documents. The Poynter Institute.

Columbia School of Journalism Records. Columbia University.

Greenfield, Meg. Papers. Library of Congress.

Geyelin, Phil. Papers. Library of Congress.

Halberstam, David. Collection. Howard Gotlieb Archival Research Center. Boston University.

McGrory, Mary. Papers. Library of Congress.

New York Times. Women's Caucus Papers. Radcliffe Institute, Harvard University. (Selected documents courtesy of Matthew Pressman.)

The Oregonian Publishing Company Records. Oregon Historical Society.

Patterson, Eugene C. Papers. The Poynter Institute. (Currently being transferred to Emory University.)

The Poynter Institute. Records.

Seib, Charles. Papers. University of Maryland, College Park.

Washington Post. Documents. Courtesy of Evelyn Small.

Oral History Interviews

The Washington Post
    Allen, Henry
    Bachrach, Judy
    Coffey, Shelby
    Downie, Leonard Jr.
    Dreyfuss, Joel
    Fisher, Marc

Frank, Jeff
Hadar, Mary
Lawrence, David
Martin, Judith
McPherson, Myra
Richard, Paul
Rosenfeld, Harry
Rosenfeld, Megan
Quinn, Sally
Secrest, Meryle
Shales, Tom
von Hoffman, Nicholas
West, Hollie

St. Petersburg Times and Poynter Institute
Clark, Roy Peter
DeGregory, Lane
Haiman, Robert
Tash, Paul

The Oregonian
Banaszynski, Jacqui
Bottomly, Therese
Hart, Jack
Rowe, Sandy

Other
DeSilva, Bruce
Fry, Don
Kramer, Mark

References
"10 That Do It Right." *Columbia Journalism Review* (March 2000): N12–N18.
Abrahamson, David. *Magazine-Made America: The Cultural Transformation of the Postwar Periodical.* Cresskill, NJ: Hampton Press, 1996.
Adam, G. Stuart. *Notes Towards a Definition of Journalism: Understanding an Old Craft as an Art Form.* Poynter Papers, no. 2. St. Petersburg, FL: Poynter Institute for Media Studies, 1993.
Altheide, David L. *Media Edge: Media Logic and Social Reality.* New York: Peter Lang, 2014.
Anderson, Chris. *Style as Argument: Contemporary American Nonfiction.* Carbondale: Southern Illinois University Press, 1987.
Applegate, Edd, ed. *Literary Journalism: A Biographical Dictionary of Writers and Editors.* Westport, CT: Greenwood Press, 1996.

Aucoin, James L. "Epistemic Responsibility and Narrative Theory: The Literary Journalism of Ryszard Kapuscinski." *Journalism* 2, no. 1 (2001): 5–21.

Babb, Laura Longley, ed. *Of the Press, by the Press, for the Press (and Others, Too): A Critical Study of the Inside Workings of the News Business, from the News Pages, Editorials, Columns, and Internal Staff Memos of the Washington Post.* Washington: Washington Post Writers Group, 1974.

———, ed. *Writing in Style: From the Style Section of the Washington Post: A New Perspective on the People and Trends of the Seventies.* Boston: Houghton Mifflin, 1975.

Bachrach, Judy. "Barbara Mandel: Time to Move On." *Washington Post*, December 21, 1973, B1.

Barkin, Steve M. "The Journalist as Storyteller: An Interdisciplinary Perspective." *American Journalism* 1, no. 2 (1984): 27–34.

Banaszynski, Jacqui. "Why We Need Stories." *Nieman Reports* (Spring 2002): 41–43.

Barnhurst, Kevin G. *Mister Pulitzer and the Spider: Modern News from Realism to the Digital.* Urbana: University of Illinois, 2016.

Barnhurst, Kevin G., and Diana Mutz. "American Journalism and the Decline in Event-Centered Reporting." *Journal of Communication* 47, no. 4 (1997): 27–53.

Barnhurst, Kevin G., and John Nerone. *The Form of News: A History.* New York: Guilford Press, 2001.

Baughman, James L. *The Republic of Mass Culture: Journalism, Filmmaking, and Broadcasting in America since 1941.* Baltimore, MD: Johns Hopkins University Press, 2006.

———. "Wounded but Not Slain: The Orderly Retreat of the American Newspaper." In *The Enduring Book: Print Culture in Postwar America*, edited by David Paul Nord, Joan Shelley Rubin, and Michael Schudson, 119–34. Chapel Hill: University of North Carolina Press, published in association with the American Antiquarian Society, 2009.

Beall, Dorothea. "Governor's Bathroom." *Washington Post*, January 12, 1969, A12.

Bennett, Lance W. *News: The Politics of Illusion.* White Plains, NY: Longman, 1996.

Benson, Rodney. "On the Explanatory and Political Uses of Journalism History." *American Journalism* 30, no. 1 (2013): 4–14.

———. *Shaping Immigration News: A French-American Comparison.* New York: Cambridge University Press, 2013.

Bernstein, Carl, and Bob Woodward. *All the President's Men.* New York: Warner Books, 1975.

Bird, S. Elizabeth. "Tabloidization: What It Is, and Does It Really Matter?" In Zelizer, *Changing Faces of Journalism*, 40–50.

Bird, S. Elizabeth, and Robert W. Dardenne. "Myth, Chronicle, and Story: Exploring the Narrative Qualities of News." In *Media, Myths, and Narratives: Television and the Press*, edited by James Carey, 67–86. Vol. 15 in the Sage Annual Reviews of Communication Research. Newbury Park, CA: Sage Publications, 1988.

———. "Rethinking News and Myth as Story-Telling." In Wahl-Jorgensen and Hanitzsch, *Handbook of Journalism Studies*, 205–17.

Blais, Madeleine. "Literary Nonfiction Constructs a Narrative Foundation." *Nieman Reports* (Fall 2000): 42–43.

Blundell, William E. *The Art and Craft of Feature Writing: Based on the Wall Street Journal Guide.* New York: New American Library, 1988.

Boczkowski, Pablo J., and Eugenia Mitchelstein. *The News Gap: When the Information Preferences of the Media and the Public Diverge.* Cambridge, MA: MIT Press, 2013.

Bogart, Leo. *Preserving the Press: How Daily Newspapers Mobilized to Keep Their Readers.* New York: Columbia University Press, 1991.

———. *Press and Public: Who Reads What, When, Where, and Why in American Newspapers.* Hillsdale, NJ: Erlbaum Associates, 1981.

Boynton, Robert S. *The New, New Journalism: Conversations with America's Best Nonfiction Writers on Their Craft.* New York: Vintage Books, 2005.

Bradlee, Ben. *A Good Life.* New York: Simon and Schuster, 1995.

Bray, Howard. *The Pillars of the Post: The Making of a News Empire in Washington.* New York: W. W. Norton, 1980.

Broersma, Marcel. *Form and Style in Journalism: European Newspapers and the Presentation of News, 1880–2005.* Leuven; Dudley, MA: Peeters, 2007.

Burke, Peter. *History and Social Theory.* 2nd ed. Ithaca: Cornell University Press, 2005.

———. *What is Cultural History?* Cambridge, UK; Malden, MA: Polity Press, 2004.

Carey, James W. "The Chicago School and the History of Mass Communication Research." In Munson and Warren, *James Carey*, 14–33.

———, ed. *Communication as Culture: Essays on Media and Society.* New York: Routledge, 2009.

———. "Communications and Economics." In Munson and Warren, *James Carey*, 60–75.

———. "A Cultural Approach to Communication." In Carey, *Communication as Culture*, 11–28.

———. "Mass Communication and Cultural Studies." In Carey, *Communication as Culture*, 29–52.

———. "The Problem of Journalism History." In Munson and Warren, *James Carey*, 88–94.

———. "'Putting the World at Peril': A Conversation with James Carey." In Munson and Warren, *James Carey*, 95–116.

Carey, James, and Lawrence Grossberg. "From New England to Illinois: The Invention of (American) Cultural Studies. James Carey in Conversation with Lawrence Grossberg, part 2." In *Thinking with James Carey: Essays on Communications, Transportation, History*, edited by Jeremy Packer and Craig Robertson, 199–225. New York: Peter Lang, 2009.

Carlson, Matt. "Introduction: The Many Boundaries of Journalism." In *Boundaries of Journalism: Professionalism, Practices, and Participation,* edited by Matt Carlson and Seth C. Lewis, 1–18. London; New York: Routledge, Taylor & Francis Group, 2015.

Chadwick, Andrew. *The Hybrid Media System: Politics and Power.* Oxford; New York: Oxford University Press, 2013.

Clark, Roy Peter, ed. *Best Newspaper Writing, 1979.* St. Petersburg, FL: Modern Media Institute, 1979.

———, ed. *Best Newspaper Writing, 1980.* St. Petersburg, FL: Modern Media Institute, 1980.

———, ed. *Best Newspaper Writing, 1981.* St. Petersburg, FL: Modern Media Institute, 1981.

———, ed. *Best Newspaper Writing, 1982.* St. Petersburg, FL: Modern Media Institute, 1982.

———, ed. *Best Newspaper Writing, 1984.* St. Petersburg, FL: The Poynter Institute, 1984.

———. "Infectious Cronkitis." *New York Times*, March 24, 1975, 31.

Clark, Roy Peter, and Christopher Scanlan, eds. *America's Best Newspaper Writing: A Collection of ASNE Prizewinners.* Boston; New York: Bedford/St. Martin's, 2001.

Cohen, Lizabeth. *A Consumers' Republic: The Politics of Mass Consumption in Postwar America.* New York: Knopf, 2003.

Connery, Thomas B. "Discovering a Literary Form." In *A Sourcebook of American Literary Journalism: Representative Writers in an Emerging Genre*, edited by Thomas B. Connery, 3–38. New York: Greenwood Press, 1992.

———. *Journalism and Realism: Rendering American Life.* Evanston, IL: Northwestern University Press, 2011.

———, ed. *A Sourcebook of American Literary Journalism: Representative Writers in an Emerging Genre.* New York: Greenwood Press, 1992.

Cook, Tim. *Governing with the News: The News Media as a Political Institution.* Chicago: University of Chicago Press, 1988.

———. "The News Media as Political Institution: Looking Backward and Looking Forward." *Political Communication* 23, no. 2 (2006): 159–71.

Corrigan, Don H. *The Public Journalism Movement in America: Evangelists in the Newsroom.* Westport, CT; London: Praeger, 1999.

Cunningham, Brent. "The Newhouse Way." *Columbia Journalism Review* (January/February 2000): 23–24.

Daly, Christopher B. *Covering America: A Narrative History of a Nation's Journalism.* Amherst: University of Massachusetts, 2012.

Darnton, Robert. "Writing News and Telling Stories." *Daedalus* 104, no. 2 (1975): 175–94.

Davies, David R. *The Postwar Decline of American Newspapers, 1945–1965: The History of American Journalism.* Westport, CT: Praeger, 2006.

Diamond, Edwin. *Behind the Times: Inside the New New York Times.* New York: Villard Books, 1993.

Dicken-Garcia, Hazel. *Journalistic Standards in Nineteenth-Century America.* Madison: University of Wisconsin Press, 1989.

Douglas, Susan. "Does Textual Analysis Tell Us Anything about Past Audiences?" In *Explorations in Communication and History*, edited by Barbie Zelizer, 66–76. London; New York: Routledge, 2008.

Driskill, Gerald W., and Angela Laird Brenton. *Organizational Culture in Action: A Cultural Analysis Workbook.* Thousand Oaks, CA: Sage Publications, 2005.

du Gay, Paul. *Doing Cultural Studies: The Story of the Sony Walkman*. London: Sage
    Publications, 1997.

Eason, David L. "The New Journalism and the Image-World." In *Literary Journal-*
    ism in the Twentieth Century, edited by Norman Sims, 191–205. New York;
    Oxford: Oxford University Press, 1990.

———. "On Journalistic Authority: The Janet Cooke Scandal." *Critical Studies in*
    Mass Communication 3, no. 4 (1986): 429–47.

Erford, Bradley T. *Research and Evaluation in Counseling*. Stamford, CT: Cengage
    Learning, 2015.

Erickson, John E. "One Approach to the Cultural History of Reporting." *Journalism*
    History 2, no. 2 (1975): 40–43.

"Exploring Jimmy's World." *Columbia Journalism Review* (July/August 1981): 28.

Fallows, James. "Big Ben." *Esquire*, April 1976, 51–54, 141–48.

Farnsworth, Stephen J., and S. Robert Lichter. *The Nightly News Nightmare: Media*
    Coverage of U.S. Presidential Elections, 1988–2008. Lanham, MD: Rowman &
    Littlefield, 2011.

Felsenthal, Carol. *Power, Privilege, and the Post: The Katharine Graham Story*. New
    York: Putnam's, 1993.

Ferree, Myra Marx, William Anthony Gamson, Jürgen Gerhards, and Dieter Rucht,
    eds. *Shaping Abortion Discourse: Democracy and the Public Sphere in Germany*
    and the United States. New York: Cambridge University Press, 2002.

Fibich, Linda. "A Brand New Ballgame." *American Journalism Review* 16, no. 9
    (November 1994): 28.

Fink, Katherine, and Michael Schudson. "The Rise of Contextual Journalism,
    1950s–2000s." *Journalism* 15, no. 1 (2014): 3–20.

Fisher Fishkin, Shelley. *From Fact to Fiction: Journalism and Imaginative Writing in*
    America. Baltimore, MD: Johns Hopkins University Press, 1985.

Fishman, Mark. *Manufacturing the News*. Austin: University of Texas Press, 1980.

Forde, Kathy Roberts. *Literary Journalism on Trial: Masson v. New Yorker and the*
    First Amendment. Amherst: University of Massachusetts Press, 2008.

Forde, Kathy Roberts, and Katharine A. Foss. "'The Facts—the Color!—the Facts':
    The Idea of a Report in American Print Culture, 1885–1910." *Book History* 15
    (2012): 123–51.

Frank, Arthur W. *Letting Stories Breathe: A Socio-Narratology*. Chicago: University
    of Chicago Press, 2010.

Franklin, Jon. *Writing for Story: Craft Secrets of Dramatic Nonfiction by a Two-Time*
    Pulitzer Prize Winner. New York: Atheneum, 1986.

Frus, Phyllis. *The Politics and Poetics of Journalistic Narrative: The Timely and Time-*
    less. Cambridge, UK; New York: Cambridge University Press, 1994.

Fulford, Robert. *The Triumph of Narrative: Storytelling in the Age of Mass Culture*.
    New York: Broadway Books, 2000.

Gans, Herbert J. *Deciding What's News: A Study of CBS Evening News, NBC Nightly*
    News, Newsweek, and Time. New York: Vintage Books, 1980.

Geertz, Clifford. *The Interpretation of Cultures: Selected Essays*. New York: Basic
    Books, 1973.

Getschow, George. "Introduction: The Best American Newspaper Narratives of 2012." In *The Best American Narratives of 2012*, edited by George Getschow, 1–12. Denton: University of North Texas Press, 2012.

Gieryn, Thomas. "Boundary-Work and the Demarcation of Science from Non-Science: Strains and Interests in Professional Ideologies of Scientists." *American Sociological Review* 48, no. 6 (1983): 781–95.

Glickman, Lawrence B. "The 'Cultural Turn.'" In *American History Now*, edited by Eric Foner and Lisa McGirr for the American Historical Association, 221–41. Philadelphia, PA: Temple University Press, 2011.

Gottlieb, Robert, and Irene Wolt. *Thinking Big: The Story of the* Los Angeles Times, *Its Publishers, and Their Influence on Southern California*. New York: G. P. Putnam's Sons, 1977.

Graham, Katharine. *Personal History*. New York: Alfred A. Knopf, 1997.

Greenwald, Marilyn. *A Woman of the Times: Journalism, Feminism, and the Career of Charlotte Curtis*. Athens: Ohio University Press, 1999.

Greenwood, Royston, Christine Oliver, Kerstin Sahlin, and Roy Suddaby, eds. *The Sage Handbook of Organizational Institutionalism*. Los Angeles: Sage Publications, 2008.

Grossberg, Lawrence. "The Conversation of Cultural Studies." *Cultural Studies* 23, no. 2 (2009): 177–82.

———. "History, Politics and Postmodernism: Stuart Hall and Cultural Studies." In *Stuart Hall: Critical Dialogues in Cultural Studies*, edited by David Morley and Kuan-Hsing Chen, 151–73. London: Routledge, 2006.

Gutkind, Lee. *The Art of Creative Nonfiction: Writing and Selling the Literature of Reality*. Wiley Books for Writers Series. New York: Wiley, 1997.

Haas, Hannes. *Empirischer Journalismus: Verfahren zur Erkundung gesellschaftlicher Wirklichkeit*. Wien: Böhlau Verlag, 1999.

Halberstam, David. *The Powers That Be*. New York: Alfred A. Knopf, 1979.

Hallin, Daniel. *We Keep America on Top of the World: Television Journalism and the Public Sphere*. London; New York: Routledge, 1994.

Hanitzsch, Thomas, and Tim P. Vos. "Journalism beyond Democracy: A New Look into Journalistic Roles in Political and Everyday Life." *Journalism* 19, no. 2 (2018): 146–64.

Hanusch, Folker. "Broadening the Focus: The Case for Lifestyle Journalism as a Field of Scholarly Inquiry." *Journalism Practice* 6, no. 1 (2012): 2–11.

Harbers, Frank, and Marcel Broersma. "Between Engagement and Ironic Ambiguity: Mediating Subjectivity in Narrative Journalism." *Journalism* 15, no. 5 (2014): 639–54.

Harp, Dustin. "Newspapers' Transition from Women's to Style Pages." *Journalism: Theory, Practice, and Criticism* 7, no. 2 (2006): 197–216.

Harrington, Walt. *Intimate Journalism: The Art and Craft of Reporting Everyday Life*. Thousand Oaks, CA: Sage Publications, 1997.

Hart, Jack. *Storycraft: The Complete Guide to Writing Narrative Nonfiction*. Chicago: University of Chicago Press, 2011.

Hartsock, John C. *A History of American Literary Journalism: The Emergence of a Modern Narrative Form*. Amherst: University of Massachusetts, 2000.

Harvey, Chris. "Tom Wolfe's Revenge." *American Journalism Review* (October 1994), retrieved from http://www.ajr.org/article.asp?id=1372.

Hellmann, John. *Fables of Fact: The New Journalism as New Fiction*. Urbana: University of Illinois, 1981.

Herman, David, ed. *The Cambridge Companion to Narrative*. Cambridge, UK; New York: Cambridge University Press, 2007.

———. "Introduction." In *The Cambridge Companion to Narrative*, edited by David Herman, 3–21. Cambridge, UK; New York: Cambridge University Press, 2007.

Heyne, Erich. "Toward a Theory of Literary Nonfiction." *MFS Modern Fiction Studies* 33, no. 3 (1987): 479–90.

Himmelman, Jeff. *Yours in Truth: A Personal Portrait of Ben Bradlee*. New York: Random House, 2012.

Hollowell John. *Fact and Fiction: The New Journalism and the Nonfiction Novel*. Chapel Hill: The University of North Carolina Press, 1977.

Hu, Winnie. "The Training Track." *American Journalism Review* 21, no. 8 (1999): 56–65.

Hughes, Helen MacGill. *News and the Human Interest Story*. New York: Greenwood Press, 1968.

Igo, Sarah E. *The Averaged American: Surveys, Citizens, and the Making of a Mass Public*. Cambridge, MA: Harvard University Press, 2008.

Kaplan, Richard L. "The News about New Institutionalism." *Political Communication* 23, no. 1 (2006): 173–85.

———. *Politics and the American Press: The Rise of Objectivity, 1865–1920*. Cambridge, UK; New York: Cambridge University Press, 2002.

Keeler, Robert F. *Newsday: A Candid History of the Respectable Tabloid*. New York: Morrow, 1990.

Kendrick, Thomas R. "Introduction." In *Writing in Style: From the Style Section of the Washington Post: A New Perspective on the People and Trends of the Seventies*, edited by Laura Longley Babb, i–xi. Boston: Houghton Mifflin, 1975.

Kernan, Michael. "Following the Master in Search of the Self." *Washington Post*, October 16, 1977.

———. "Life Styles: The Mandels of Maryland." *Washington Post*, January 8, 1969.

Kessler, Lauren. *The Dissident Press: Alternative Journalism in American History*. Beverly Hills, CA: Sage Publications, 1984.

Kimball, Penn. "A Multiple Embarrassment." *Columbia Journalism Review* (July/ August 1981): 34–36.

Kitch, Carolyn. "A News of Feeling as Well as Fact: Mourning and Memorial in American Newsmagazines." *Journalism* 1, no. 2 (2000): 171–95.

———. "Tears and Trauma in the News." In Zelizer, *Changing Faces of Journalism*, 29–39.

Kleinman, Sherryl, and Martha A. Copp. *Emotions and Fieldwork*. Newbury Park, CA: Sage Publications, 1993.

Kluger, Richard, and Phyllis Kluger. *The Paper: The Life and Death of the New York Herald Tribune*. New York: Alfred A. Knopf, 1986.

Kovach, Bill, and Tom Rosenstiel. *The Elements of Journalism: What Newspeople Should Know and the Public Should Expect*. New York: Crown Publishers, 2001.

Kramer, Mark. "Narrative Journalism Comes of Age." *Nieman Reports* (Fall 2000): 5–6.

Kristensen, Nete Nørgaard, and Unni From. "From Ivory Tower to Cross-Media Personas: The Heterogeneous Cultural Critic in the Media." *Journalism Practice* 9, no. 6 (2015): 853–71.

Laakaniemi, Ray. "An Analysis of Writing Coach Programs on American Daily Newspapers." *Journalism and Mass Communication Quarterly* 64, nos. 2–3 (1985): 569–75.

Lacy, Stephen, and Lucinda Davenport. "Daily Newspaper Market Structure, Concentration, and Competition." *Journal of Media Economics* 7, no. 3 (1994): 33–46.

Lambeth, Edmund B., Philip E. Meyer, and Esther Thorson, eds. *Assessing Public Journalism*. Columbia, MO: University of Missouri Press, 1998.

Latham, Aaron. "Waking Up with Sally Quinn." *New York*, July 16, 1973, 22–29.

Laventhol, David. "*Washington Post* Thinks Style Is Stylish." American Society of Newspaper Editors. *Bulletin of the American Society of Newspaper Editors*, no. 533 (August 1969).

Lazerow, Jama. "1960–1974." In *A Companion to 20th-Century America*, edited by Stephen J. Whitfield, 87–101. Malden, MA: Blackwell Publishing, 2004.

Lehman, Daniel W. *Matters of Fact: Reading Nonfiction over the Edge*. Columbus: Ohio State University Press, 1997.

Leland, Timothy. "Lilt and Lyricism on the News Pages." *Boston Globe*, May 12, 1978.

Leonard, Thomas C. *News for All: America's Coming-of-Age with the Press*. New York: Oxford University Press, 1995.

Limpert, Jack. "David Laventhol, Ben Bradlee, and the Rise and Fall of Style." *About Editing and Writing* (blog), jacklimpert.com, April 10, 2015, http://jacklimpert.com/2015/04/david-laventhol-rise-fall-style/.

Lisheron, Mark. "Riding High." *American Journalism Review* (March 2000): 34–40.

Lounsberry, Barbara. *The Art of Fact: Contemporary Artists of Nonfiction*. New York: Greenwood Press, 1990.

Lowndes, Vivien, and Mark Roberts. *Why Institutions Matter: The New Institutionalism in Political Science*. Houndmills, Basingstoke, Hampshire: Palgrave Macmillan, 2013.

Lule, Jack. *Daily News, Eternal Stories: The Mythological Role of Journalism*. New York: Guilford Press, 2001.

Macdonald, Dwight. "Parajournalism, or Tom Wolfe and His Magic Writing Machine." In *The Reporter as Artist: A Look at the New Journalism Controversy*, edited by Ronald Weber, 223–33. New York: Hastings House Publishers, 1980.

Maier, Thomas. *Newhouse: All the Glitter, Power, and Glory of America's Richest Media Empire and the Secretive Man behind It.* New York: St. Martin's Press, 1994.

March, James G., and Johan P. Olsen. *Rediscovering Institutions: The Organizational Basis of Politics.* New York: The Free Press, 1989.

Martin, Judith. "Before You Look Too Far Down Your Nose at 'Women's Pages,' Judith Martin Has a Word for You." *Washington Post Magazine,* December 12, 2014.

Marzolf, Marion. "Operationalizing Carey: An Approach to the Cultural History of Journalism." *Journalism History* 2, no. 2 (1975): 42–43.

McChesney, Robert W. *The Political Economy of Media: Enduring Issues, Emerging Dilemmas.* New York: Monthly Review Press, 2008.

McManus, John H. "The Commercialization of News." In Wahl-Jorgensen and Hanitzsch, *Handbook of Journalism Studies,* 218–36.

Melzer, Helene. "Ben, Where Are You Hiding the *Post* Women's Section?" *Washingtonian,* April 1969, 53.

Mills, Kay. *A Place in the News: From the Women's Pages to the Front Page.* New York: Dodd, Mead, 1988.

Mindich, David T. Z. *Just the Facts: How "Objectivity" Came to Define American Journalism.* New York: New York University Press, 1998.

Mirando, Joseph A. "Lessons On Ethics in News Reporting Textbooks, 1867–1997." *Journal of Mass Media Ethics* 13, no. 1 (1998): 26–39.

Molotch, Harvey, and Marilyn Lester. "Accidental News: The Great Oil Spill as Local Occurrence and National Event." *American Journal of Sociology* 81, no. 2 (1975): 235–60.

Morrissey, Charles T. "Oral History and Archives: Documenting Context." in *Handbook of Oral History,* edited by Thomas L. Charlton, Lois E. Myers, and Rebecca Sharpless, 170–206. Lanham, MD: Altamira Press, 2006.

Munson, Eve Stryker, and Catherine A. Warren, eds. *James Carey: A Critical Reader.* Minneapolis: University of Minnesota Press, 1997.

Nadler, Anthony M. *Making the News Popular: Mobilizing U.S. News Audiences.* Urbana: University of Illinois Press, 2016.

Nerone, John J. "Narrative News Story." In *The International Encyclopedia of Communication,* ed. Wolfgang Donsbach. Accessed May 15, 2013. https://doi .org/10.1002/9781405186407.wbiecn002.

Nielsen, Rasmus Kleis. *Ten Years That Shook the Media World.* Oxford: Reuters Institute for the Study of Journalism, 2012.

Nieman Foundation. "Talking about Narrative Journalism." *Nieman Reports* (Fall 2000): 20–22.

Noah, Timothy. "What David Broder Could Learn from Sally Quinn (and Vice Versa)." *Washington Monthly,* December 1984, 13.

Nord, David Paul. "James Carey and Journalism History." *Journalism History* 32, no. 3 (2006): 122–27.

North Central Publishing Company. *Fifty and Feisty: APME, 1933 to 1983.* St. Paul, MN: North Central Publishing Company, 1983.

Patterson, James T. *Grand Expectations: The United States, 1945–1974*. New York: Oxford University Press, 1996.

Patterson, Thomas E. *Out of Order*. New York: A. Knopf, 1993.

Pauly, John J. "The New Journalism and the Struggle for Interpretation." *Journalism* 15, no. 5 (2014): 589–604.

———. "The Politics of the New Journalism." In *Literary Journalism in the Twentieth Century*, edited by Norman Sims, 110–32. New York; Oxford: Oxford University Press, 1990.

Peters, Chris. "Emotion Aside or Emotional Side? Crafting an 'Experience of Involvement' in the News." *Journalism* 13, no. 3 (2011): 297–316.

Peters, John Durham. "Technology and Ideology: The Case of the Telegraph Revisited." In *Thinking with James Carey: Essays on Communications, Transportation, History*, edited by Jeremy Packer and Craig Robertson, 137–56. New York: Peter Lang, 2009.

Picard, Robert G. *The Economics and Financing of Media Companies*. 2nd ed. New York: Fordham University Press, 2012.

———. *Media Economics: Concepts and Issues*. New York: Sage Publications, 1987.

———. "Twilight or New Dawn of Journalism? Evidence from the Changing News Ecosystem." *Journalism Studies* 15, no. 5 (2014): 273–83.

Polumbaum, Judy. "Human Interest Journalism." In *Encyclopedia of Journalism*, edited by Christopher H. Sterling, 729–32. Thousand Oaks, CA: Sage Publications, 2009.

Pooley, Jefferson. *James W. Carey and Communication Research: Reputation at the University's Margins*. New York: Peter Lang, 2016.

Portelli, Alessandro. "The Peculiarities of Oral History." *History Workshop* 12 (1981): 96–106.

Pöttker, Horst. "News and Its Communicative Quality: The Inverted Pyramid—When and Why Did It Appear?." *Journalism Studies* 4, no. 4 (2003): 501–11.

Pratte, Paul Alfred. *Gods within the Machine: A History of the American Society of Newspaper Editors, 1923–1993*. Westport, CT: Praeger, 1995.

Pressman, Matthew. "Remaking the News: The Transformation of American Journalism, 1960–1980." PhD diss., Boston University, 2016.

Prior, Lindsay. *Using Documents in Social Research*. London: Sage Publications, 2003.

Quinn, Sally. *We Are Going to Make You a Star*. New York: Simon and Schuster, 1975.

Richardson, John E. *Language and Journalism*. London; New York: Routledge, 2010.

Ritchie, Donald A. *Reporting from Washington: The History of the Washington Press Corps*. Oxford; New York: Oxford University Press, 2005.

Roberts, Chalmers M. *The Washington Post: The First 100 Years*. Boston: Houghton Mifflin, 1977.

Roessner, Amber, Rick Popp, Brian Creech, and Fred Blevens. "'A Measure of The-
    ory?': Considering the Role of Theory in Media History." *American Journalism*
    30, no. 2 (2013): 260–78.
Rosenfeld, Harry. *From Kristallnacht to Watergate: Memoirs of a Newspaperman.*
    Albany: State University of New York Press, 2013.
Rowe, Sandra Mims. "Why Series Matter." *American Journalism Review* (September
    2001): 40–41.
Rupar, Verica. *Journalism and Meaning-Making: Reading the Newspaper.* Cresskill,
    NJ: Hampton Press, 2010.
Ryfe, David. *Can Journalism Survive?: An inside Look at American Newsrooms.*
    Cambridge, UK; Malden, MA: Polity Press, 2012.
———. "Introduction." *Political Communication* 23, no. 1 (2006): 135–44.
Sachs, Jonah. *Winning the Story Wars: Why Those Who Tell—and Live—the Best
    Stories Will Rule the Future.* Boston: Harvard Business Review Press, 2012.
"Sandra Mims Rowe: She Just Wins." *Columbia Journalism Review* 2001 (Novem-
    ber/December 2001): 124.
Schmidt, Thomas R. "Michael Kernan: Poet and Newspaperman." Presentation,
    IALJS 10 (International Association for Literary Journalism Studies), Univer-
    sity of St. Thomas, Minneapolis, May 7–9, 2015.
Schneiberg, Marc, and Michael Lounsbury. "Social Movements and Institutional
    Analysis." In *The Sage Handbook of Organizational Institutionalism,* edited
    by Royston Greenwood, Christine Oliver, Kerstin Sahlin, and Roy Suddaby,
    650–72. Thousand Oaks, CA: Sage Publications, 2008.
Schor, Juliet. *The Overspent American: Upscaling, Downshifting, and the New Con-
    sumer.* New York: Basic Books, 1998.
Schudson, Michael. *Discovering the News: A Social History of American Newspapers.*
    New York: Basic Books, 1978.
———. "Four Approaches to the Sociology of News." In *Mass Media and Society,*
    edited by James Curran and Michael Gurevitch, 172–97. 4th ed. London:
    Hodder Arnold, 2005.
———. "Fourteen or Fifteen Generations: News as a Cultural Form and Journalism
    as a Historical Formation." *American Journalism* 30, no. 1 (2013): 29–35.
———. *The Rise of the Right to Know: Politics and the Culture of Transparency,
    1945–1975.* Cambridge, MA: Belknap Press of Harvard University, 2015.
———. *The Sociology of News.* New York: W. W. Norton, 2003.
Schulman, Bruce J. *The Seventies: The Great Shift in American Culture, Society, and
    Politics.* New York: Free Press, 2001.
Schwarzlose, Richard A. "First Things First: A Proposal." *Journalism History* 2, no. 2
    (1975): 38–39; 63.
Scott, John. *A Matter of Record: Documentary Sources in Social Research.* Cam-
    bridge, UK: Polity Press; Cambridge: B. Blackwell, 1990.
Self, Robert O. *All in the Family: The Realignment of American Democracy since the
    1960s.* New York: Hill and Wang, 2012.
Shaw, David. "Smoothing Out the First Rough Draft of History." *Washington Jour-
    nalism Review* (December 1981): 28–34.

Sherrill, Martha. "Ben Bradlee: His Sense of Style Brought a New Sensibility to Features." *Washington Post*, October 21, 2014.

Sims, Norman. *The Literary Journalists*. New York: Ballantine Books, 1984.

———. *True Stories: A Century of Literary Journalism*. Evanston, IL: Northwestern University Press, 2007.

Sims, Norman, and Mark Kramer, eds. *Literary Journalism: A New Collection of the Best American Nonfiction*. New York: Ballantine Books, 1995.

Soderlund, Gretchen. "Communication Scholarship as Ritual: An Examination of James Carey's Cultural Model of Communication." In *Thinking with James Carey: Essays on Communications, Transportation, History*, edited by Jeremy Packer and Craig Robertson, 101–16. New York: Peter Lang, 2009.

Sparks, Colin, and John Tulloch. *Tabloid Tales: Global Debates over Media Standards*. Lanham, MD: Rowan and Littlefield, 2000.

Sparrow, Bartholomew H. *Uncertain Guardians: The News Media as a Political Institution*. Baltimore, MD: Johns Hopkins University Press, 1999.

Startt, James D., and Wm. David Sloan. *Historical Methods in Mass Communication*. Hillsdale, NJ: L. Erlbaum Associates, 1989.

Steensen, Steen. "The Intimization of Journalism." In *The Sage Handbook of Digital Journalism*, edited by Tamara Witschge, C. W. Anderson, David Domingo, and Alfred Hermida, 111–27. London: Sage Publications, 2016.

Steiner, Linda. "Construction of Gender in News Reporting Textbooks: 1890–1990." Journalism Monograph 135. Columbia, SC: Association for Education in Journalism and Mass Communication, 1992.

Stepp, Carl Sessions. "The State of the American Newspaper: Then and Now." *American Journalism Review* 21, no. 7 (1999): 60–75.

Streitmatter, Rodger. "Transforming the Women's Pages: Strategies That Worked." *Journalism History* 24, no. 2 (1998): 72–81.

Strömbäck, Jesper, and Susana Salgado. "Interpretive Journalism: A Review of Concepts, Operationalizations, and Key Findings." *Journalism* 13, no. 2 (2012): 144–61.

Sugrue, Thomas J. *Origins of the Urban Crisis: Race and Inequality in Postwar Detroit*. Princeton, NJ: Princeton University Press, 1996.

Tenenboim-Weinblatt, Keren. "News as Narrative." In *Encyclopedia of Journalism*, edited by Christopher H. Sterling, 953–56. Thousand Oaks, CA: Sage Publications, 2009.

Tucher, Andie. "Notes on a Cultural History of Reporting." *Cultural Studies* 23, no. 2 (2009): 289–98.

———. "Why Journalism History Matters: The Gaffe, the 'Stuff,' and the Historical Imagination." *American Journalism* 31, no. 4 (2014): 432–44.

Tuchman, Gaye. *Making News: A Study in the Construction of Reality*. New York: Free Press, 1978.

Turow, Joseph. *Breaking up America: Advertisers and the New Media World*. Chicago: University of Chicago Press, 1997.

Underwood, Doug. *When MBAs Rule the Newsroom: How the Marketers and Managers are Reshaping Today's Media*. New York: Columbia University Press, 1993.

———. "When MBAs Rule the Newsroom," *Columbia Journalism Review* (March/ April 1988), 23.

Usher, Nikki. *Interactive Journalism: Hackers, Data, and Code.* Urbana: University of Illinois Press, 2016.

von Hoffman, Nicholas. "Mule Wagon Leads March." *Washington Post*, April 10, 1968.

———. "Women's Pages: An Irreverent View." *Columbia Journalism Review* (July/ August 1971): 52–54.

Vos, Tim. "Historical Mechanisms and Journalistic Change." *American Journalism* 30, no. 1 (2013): 36–43.

Voss, Kimberly Wilmot. "Redefining Women's News: A Case Study of Three Women's Page Editors and Their Framing of the Women's Movement." PhD diss., University of Maryland, College Park, 2004.

Wahl-Jorgensen, Karin. "The Strategic Ritual of Emotionality: A Case Study of Pulitzer Prize–Winning Articles." *Journalism* 14, no. 1 (2013): 129–45.

———. "Subjectivity and Story-Telling in Journalism: Examining Expressions of Affect, Judgment, and Appreciation in Pulitzer Prize–Winning Stories." *Journalism Studies* 14, no. 3 (2013): 305–20.

Wahl-Jorgensen, Karin, and Thomas Hanitzsch, *The Handbook of Journalism Studies.* 2nd ed. New York: Routledge, 2009.

Wahl-Jorgensen, Karin, and Thomas R. Schmidt, "News and Storytelling." In Wahl-Jorgensen and Hanitzsch, *Handbook of Journalism Studies.*

Wanta, Wayne, and Thomas Johnson. "Content Changes in the St. Louis Post-Dispatch During Different Market Situations." *Journal of Media Economics* 7, no. 1 (1994): 13–28.

Weingarten, Marc. *The Gang That Wouldn't Write Straight: Wolfe, Thompson, Didion, and the New Journalism Revolution.* New York: Crown Publishers, 2006.

Weldon, Michele. *Everyman News: The Changing American Front Page.* Columbia: University of Missouri Press, 2007.

Wicker, Tom. "The Greening of the Press," *Columbia Journalism Review* 10, no. 1 (May/June 1971): 12.

Williams, Bruce Alan, and Michael X. Delli Carpini. *After Broadcast News: Media Regimes, Democracy, and the New Information Environment.* New York: Cambridge University Press, 2011.

Wills, Garry. *Lead Time: A Journalist's Education.* Garden City, NY: Doubleday, 1983.

Wilson, Christopher P. *The Labor of Words: Literary Professionalism in the Progressive Era.* Athens: University of Georgia Press, 1985.

———. *Reading Narrative Journalism: An Introduction for Students.* Boston College. 2017. https://mediakron.bc.edu/readingnarrativejournalism/home.

Wolfe, Tom. "The New Journalism." In *The New Journalism*, edited by Tom Wolfe and E. W. Johnson, 1–36. New York: Harper & Row, 1973.

Woo, William. "Just Write What Happened." *Nieman Reports* (Fall 2000): 16–17.

Wood, Gordon S. *The Purpose of the Past: Reflections on the Uses of History.* New York: Penguin Press, 2008.

Yang, Mei-Ling. "Women's Pages or People's Pages: The Production of News for Women in the *Washington Post* in the 1950s." *Journalism and Mass Communication Quarterly* 73, no. 2 (1996): 364–78.

Yodelis Smith, MaryAnn. "The Method of History." In *Research Methods in Mass Communication*, edited by Guido H. Stempel III and Bruce H. Westley, 316–30. 2nd ed. Englewood Cliffs, NJ: Prentice Hall, 1989.

Zelizer, Barbie. "Achieving Journalistic Authority through Narrative." *Critical Studies in Mass Communication* 7, no. 4 (1990): 366–76.

———, ed. *The Changing Faces of Journalism: Tabloidization, Technology, and Truthiness*. New York: Routledge, 2009.

———. "Introduction: Why Journalism's Changing Faces Matter." In Zelizer, *Changing Faces of Journalism*, 1–10.

———. "Jim Carey's Book of the Dead." *Cultural Studies* 23, no. 2 (2009): 299–303.

———. *Taking Journalism Seriously: News and the Academy*. Thousand Oaks, CA: Sage Publications, 2004.

Index

Nieman Foundation, 99
Nieman Reports, 100
Nixon, Richard, 31
Nohlgren, Steve, 55–56
Norfolk Ledger-Star, 87
Northeast Mississippi Daily Journal, 71, 73
Northwestern University, 103

obedient press, 60, 116
objectivity, as professional ideology of
    journalism, 3, 49, 53, 68, 75–76, 108,
    112
Oliphant, Thomas, 67
Oregonian, 78, 86–97, 98
Orlando Sentinel Star, 62, 134n56

Patterson, Eugene C., 67; as ASNE
    president, 60–61; at the *St. Petersburg
    Times*, 51–54; at the *Washington Post*,
    35–36, 40, 44
Pauly, John J., 75
Penney-Missouri Journalism Awards, 73
Pentagon Papers, 31
Pett, Saul, 68
Philadelphia Inquirer, 4, 67, 71–72, 77
Phillips, B.J., 32
Picard, Robert, 104
political economy, 104, 110
Porter, Don, 64
Poynter Institute, 4, 62, 73, 74, 89, 90, 91,
    97, 114
Pride, Mike, 72
Pulitzer Prize, 69, 72, 74–75, 91, 94, 95,
    96, 99, 114; for feature writing, 43–45,
    66

Quinn, Sally, 32, 36–37

race relations, 34–35, 116
Ragdale, James, 59
Raleigh News and Observer, 59, 84
Raleigh Times, 59, 84
Read, Rich, 96
readership project, 60

readership studies, 103
Reading (PA) Eagle and Times, 134n56
realism, 112
Redwood City Tribune, 32
Remnick, David, 42
Richman, Alan, 62
Rinnearson, Richard, 69
Riverside (CA) Press-Enterprise, 47–48
Roberts, Chalmers, 31
Roberts, Eugene L., 72
Rolling Stone magazine, 18
Rosenfeld, Megan, 32
Rowe, Sandra Mims, 87, 91–92, 93–94,
    95, 96
Ryfe, David, 109, 138n17

Sacramento Bee, 71–73, 132n20
Salgado, Susana, 107
San Jose Mercury News, 77
Sauer, Marie, 19, 23
Scanlan, Christopher (Chip), 93, 99
Schudson, Michael, 4, 9, 53, 104–5, 111,
    121n9, 143n36
Seattle Times, 69
sensationalism, 8, 48, 70
service journalism, 83–84
sexism, 19, 33
sexual revolution, 22
Shreveport (LA) Times, 136n100
Sitton, Claude, 59
Smith, June, 134n56
Smith, Patricia, 94
soft news, 8, 19, 23, 26, 42, 48, 70, 80, 114,
    117. See also human interest stories
Southern Newspaper Publishers
    Association (SNPA), 133n55, 134n56
Sparrow, Bartholomew, H., 109
Spokesman Review and Spokane Chronicle,
    86
St. Petersburg Times, 20, 51–58, 60, 61, 84,
    85, 90
State University of New York at Stony
    Brook, 52
status details, 25, 72

Steensen, Steen, 121n7
Stepp, Carl Sessions, 106
Stern, Lawrence, 31
story form, 24–25, 48
Strömbäck, Jesper, 107
Suhre, Lawrence, 134n56
Sullivan, Julie, 86

tabloidism, 48, 70
Talese, Gay, 4, 5, 28, 36, 121n7
Tampa Bay Times. See St. Petersburg
    Times
Tatarian, Roger, 134n56
television, influence of, 16, 23, 27, 41, 56,
    66, 82, 94, 105, 114
Tenenboim-Weinblatt, Keren, 7–8,
    143n38
Thompson, Hunter S., 4, 5, 27
Time magazine, 20, 24, 26
Tucher, Andie, 37

Underwood, Doug, 80–81
Ungaro, Joe, 134n56
University of Hawaii, 132n20
University of Missouri, 4, 99
University of New Hampshire, 62
University of Oregon School of
    Journalism and Mass Communication,
    87, 99
University of Wisconsin, 87
upscaling of newspapers, 78, 81, 103

Vietnam, war in, 16, 40
Virginian-Pilot, 87
Visalia Times-Delta, 47
Vos, Tim, 10, 49

Wahl-Jorgensen, Karin, 74–75
Wald, Dick, 27
Wall Street Journal, 64
Walston, John, 97
Washington City Paper, 98

Washington Daily, 16–17
Washington, DC, 17–18
Washington Post, 4, 11, 15–45, 51, 58,
    107; Janet Cooke scandal, 63–66; letters
    to the editor, 37–40; 64; newsroom
    culture, 31–37; women's section, 18–25,
    33, 38, 41, 107. See also *Washington
    Post* Style section
Washington Post Style section, 4, 11–12,
    15–45, 67–68, 81, 82–83, 85
Washington Star, 16–17, 65
Washington Times-Herald, 43
watchdog journalism, 77
Watergate, 31
Watertown (NY) Daily Times, 136n100
Weldon, Michelle, 11, 106
West, Hollie, 34
Westchester-Rockland Newspapers, 134n56
Wicker, Tom, 35
Wiggins, Russel, 58
Williams, Nick, 20
Wilson, Christopher P., 5, 29, 80, 111
Winburn, Jan, 85
Wolfe, Tom, 4, 5, 25, 27, 28, 35, 36, 54, 72,
    97–98, 121n7
women, changing role of, 18, 116–17
women's movement, 16, 19, 22, 33
women's section in newspapers, 19, 26, 32.
    See also *Washington Post* Style section
Woo, William, 100
Wood, David, 62, 133n56
Woodward, Bob, 42
writing coaches, 4, 62, 72, 73, 74, 82, 87,
    88, 90, 114, 132n20, 134n56, 136n102
writing movement. *See* narrative writing
    movement

yellow journalism, 40

Zahler, Richard, 69
Zelizer, Barbie, 6, 110
Zucchino, David, 69

About the Author

Thomas R. Schmidt is an assistant professor of critical journalism studies at the University of California, San Diego.

Photo by Heather Norris